EUREKA!
discoveries

KINGFISHER

EUREKA!
discoveries

CLAIRE LLEWELLYN

Designed and edited by Bookwork Ltd

Art editor: Kate Mullins
Art director: Jill Plank
Editorial director: Louise Pritchard

For Kingfisher

Senior editor: Catherine Brereton
Senior designer: Malcolm Parchment
Picture research manager: Cee Weston-Baker
Production controller: Jessamy Oldfield
DTP co-ordinator: Jonathan Pledge
Artwork archivists: Wendy Allison, Jenny Lord

KINGFISHER

Kingfisher Publications Plc,
New Penderel House,
283–288 High Holborn,
London WC1V 7HZ

www.kingfisherpub.com

First published by
Kingfisher Publications Plc in 2004

2 4 6 8 10 9 7 5 3 1
1TR/0704/SNP/PICA/150MA

A CIP catalogue record for this book
is available from the British Library.

ISBN 0 7534 0974 7

Printed in China

CONTENTS

EUREKA!
*A dramatic moment of discovery is known as a
'eureka' moment after the shout of the Greek
scientist Archimedes (287–212BCE). He was in the
bath, thinking about a scientific problem, when
he had a brainwave. He was so excited about
his sudden realization that he jumped out of his
bath and ran naked through his city, shouting
"Eureka!" – Greek for "I've got it!". This book
tells the stories of other thrilling 'eureka' moments.*

Foreword

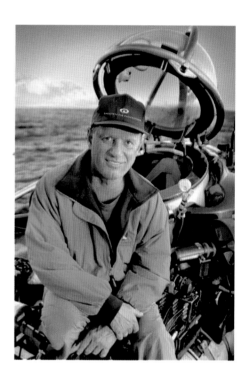

'The deep sea is a great
preserver of human history,
a giant museum waiting for the
next generation of explorers.'

I have been very fortunate to participate in a number of great discoveries and
amazing adventures in the deep sea. Some involved the exploration of nature's
wonder beneath the sea, while others involved discoveries of lost chapters of
human history.

My love of adventure in the sea stems from an early childhood interest in Jules
Verne's classic *20,000 Leagues Under the Sea,* featuring the adventures of Captain
Nemo and his crew aboard their mythical submarine the *Nautilus.* As a child
watching the movie version of the book, I made an amazing discovery that
changed my life forever and helped make me who I am today. The story begins
with a battle between the *Nautilus* and a British warship sent to kill what its crew
thinks is a great sea monster. The morning after the warship has been rammed
and sunk by the *Nautilus,* a surviving crew member climbs aboard the *Nautilus*
to discover that no one is aboard. Then he looks out of one of the sub's giant
viewports to see Captain Nemo and crew walking on the bottom of the ocean.
Walking, I thought! I had thought about swimming, sailing, surfing, but never
had I thought about walking on the bottom of the ocean.

From that day forward my view of the ocean changed. I was fascinated with the
bottom of the ocean and when I heard that the greatest mountain ranges on earth
were beneath the sea, I had to see them. In fact, I was one of the first human
beings to explore the Mid-Ocean Ridge, the largest mountain range on earth.

It runs around the earth like the seam on a baseball or cricket ball, stretching for a distance of 70,000km. While exploring deep-sea mountain ranges in the mid 1970s we made even greater discoveries, new life forms that live not off the energy of the sun like plants and animals, but off the energy of the earth, through a process we now call chemosynthesis. There, in the rift valley of the Mid-Ocean Ridge, we discovered amazing giant tubeworms, some one-and-a-half metres tall with human-like blood inside their bodies, and masses of bacteria, living inside the worms, carrying out the process of producing food and energy in total darkness.

That was just the beginning of my discoveries beneath the sea. Just a few years later, our team would discover the final resting place of the British luxury liner *RMS Titanic* resting in its watery grave some 3,500m under the icy waters of the North Atlantic. And then we discovered the German battleship *Bismarck* in even deeper water, followed by many other lost ships. Those discoveries led to more, as we looked back even farther and farther into time, discovering ancient shipwrecks in the deep sea where no one thought they would be found, some more than 2,700 years old. Now we realize that the deep sea is a great preserver of human history, a giant museum waiting for the next generation of explorers to find hundreds of thousands of lost treasures. What is important to remember is that the generation of explorers who are at school right now will explore more of the earth beneath the sea – which covers 72 per cent of the globe's surface – than all previous generations combined. And that holds true also in outer space and within the human body and mind. So as you enjoy this wonderful book of amazing finds, lost cities and sunken treasure, pause for a moment and think about the adventures and discoveries that are awaiting you.

Dr Robert Ballard

Nature's marvels

Until a chance discovery about 180 years ago,
no one knew about the giant reptiles of the past.
The word 'dinosaur' had not even been invented.
The earth conceals many clues to its millions of years
of history, but sometimes these clues come to light,
and some amazing finds have been made in its
deserts, rocks, bogs and seas. More and more
prehistoric creatures have been uncovered, ancient
creatures believed to be extinct have turned up alive
and well, and human remains up to 4,000 years
old have been found miraculously preserved.
These major discoveries by curious scientists have
changed our understanding of life on earth.

Huge reptiles from the past

The *Iguanodon* teeth identified by Gideon Mantell

F or hundreds of years, people dug up huge dinosaur fossils without understanding what they really were. Some people thought they were the bones of dragons; others believed they belonged to giant buffaloes. Then, in 1824, an English doctor made a major discovery when he identified the true owner of some huge fossilized teeth.

THE DOCTOR

Gideon Mantell (1790–1852), a doctor in the south of England, was a keen fossil collector. In 1822, he was visiting a patient while his wife waited outside. She spotted some fossils in a pile of stones and picked them up. When she showed them to her husband, he thought they were the teeth of an elephant or another big plant-eater.

DETECTIVE WORK

Mantell wanted to find out what the fossils were. He tracked down their original source to a nearby quarry, where the rocks were about 130 million years old. No large mammals were alive that long ago, so what sort of animal could the teeth have belonged to? Mantell continued investigating the unusual fossils.

! DINOSAURS

Mantell's deduction that huge reptiles had existed in the remote past began a worldwide fascination with dinosaurs. The word dinosaur, meaning 'terrible lizard', was coined by another British scientist, Richard Owen (1804–1892), about 20 years later.

A GIANT LIZARD

Mantell searched through collections of animal skeletons, looking for anything that matched the fossilized teeth. At last he found identical teeth in the much smaller jaw of a modern iguana – a species of lizard. *Eureka!* Mantell realized that the prehistoric teeth came from a giant lizard, possibly a huge iguana, that was now extinct. He published a description of the teeth and named the animal *Iguanodon*, which means 'iguana tooth'. Mantell's discovery challenged the Church, which taught that God's creation was perfect, so animals would never become extinct. His findings began to change these views and led to a proper understanding of dinosaurs and the prehistoric world.

'Now for three months' hard work with my chisel…'

DR GIDEON MANTELL
Amateur fossil collector

Iguanodon with the smaller
Deinonychus, a fierce predator

Scientists found out more about **Iguanodon** *when, 50 years after Mantell's discovery, nearly 30 complete fossilized skeletons of the animal were found in Belgium.* Iguanodon *lived in warm forests about 100 million years ago. It measured up to 10m long and had smooth, scaly skin. It moved around on its hind legs and fed on trees and other plants. It had a sharp, horny spike on its thumb, which it used to defend itself against predators.*

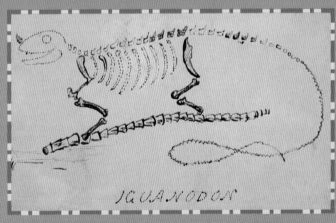

IGUANODON

A sketch by Gideon Mantell of how *Iguanodon* may have looked

THE RECONSTRUCTION

Nine years after Mantell's discovery, a large jumble of *Iguanodon* bones was discovered in a slab of rock in a quarry in Kent in southeast England. Mantell's friends bought the bones for him for £25. Mantell spent months chiselling the bones apart and making sketches to show how they may have fitted together. His ideas proved to be very inaccurate. For example, he drew the dinosaur's thumb spike on the end of its nose!

Fossil of an ancient bird

In the mid 19th century CE, scientists were learning more about prehistoric life. They grew curious about how ancient creatures related to living animals. Some believed that during the earth's long history, animals had changed in a process called evolution. Others believed they had stayed the same. Then a new fossil was discovered. Scientific understanding was about to take a major step forwards.

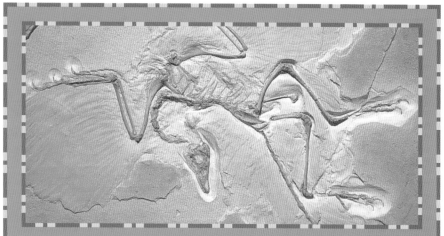

Archaeopteryx fossil found in 1861, now in the Natural History Museum, London, UK

JURASSIC BIRD

The fossil of *Archaeopteryx* was found inside a slab of limestone dating from the Jurassic Period, about 147 million years ago. This makes it the earliest known bird. The skeleton shows the teeth, claws and long, bony tail of a reptile, and the feathers and wishbone of a bird. The fossil is now kept in environmentally controlled conditions in the Natural History Museum in London. It is so fragile and valuable that it is rarely on public display.

! ARCHAEOPTERYX
The discovery of this rare fossil caused a stir in scientific circles and led to a breakthrough in our understanding of evolution. Scientists began to examine the links between reptiles and birds and concluded that birds evolved from small, meat-eating dinosaurs about 150 million years ago.

REPTILE OR BIRD?

In 1861, a quarryman was working in a limestone quarry in Bavaria, southern Germany, when he found an unusual fossil of a bird-like reptile. He gave it to his doctor Karl Haberlein in payment of a medical bill. Haberlein was an amateur fossil collector. He realized that the fossil was special and showed it to a professor of geology. The professor then stunned the scientific world by announcing that this was the fossil of a primitive bird. He named it *Archaeopteryx*, from the Greek for 'ancient wing'.

SCIENTIFIC DEBATE

A year later, Dr Haberlein needed money for his daughter's wedding. So he sold the *Archaeopteryx* fossil to the Natural History Museum in London for £450, a huge sum at the time. The fossil could not have arrived at a more controversial time. The English scientist Charles Darwin (1809–1882) had just published his book *On the Origin of Species*, in which he argued his belief that, to survive in a changing world, animal species either died out or evolved. Many scientists opposed this theory. Known as pro-creationists, they supported the Church's teaching that all species of animal were created by God. *Archaeopteryx* became a major part of the debate.

This is how scientists believe *Archaeopteryx* may have looked when it was alive.

Archaeopteryx *was about the size of a crow. It had well-developed feathers, teeth and three long toes with claws. It had clawed fingers on its wings, which it may have used to grasp prey.*

AN EXCITING NEW THEORY

The pro-creationists said that *Archaeopteryx* was simply an ancient, long-tailed bird. Darwin's supporters said it was more. In 1868, the English scientist Thomas Huxley (1825–1895) argued that birds and reptiles shared so many features that they must be related. *Eureka!* The fossil of *Archaeopteryx* was the proof. With its reptile teeth and bird feathers, it was a species in the process of evolutionary change. Recent finds support this idea. Fossils from about 123 million years ago have been found in China. With dinosaur-like skeletons and bird feathers, these 'dino-birds' are similar to *Archaeopteryx*.

An Iron Age human sacrifice

H uman remains decay quickly after death, so it is unlikely that a person's body will survive in the ground for 2,000 years. Yet this is what happened in one remarkable case in Denmark. In 1950, the perfectly preserved, 2,000-year-old body of a man was discovered in a peat bog at Tollund Fen. He became known as Tollund Man. But who was he, and how did he die?

When two Danish peat-cutters uncovered the face of a man in a peat bog, they thought he was a recent murder victim and notified the police. Knowing that ancient remains sometimes turned up in the bog, the police brought experts to the scene. *Eureka!* They discovered that the man was about 2,000 years old. They dug him up, packed him in a crate and sent him to the National Museum in Copenhagen.

Tollund Man's *peaceful expression belies his violent end. He was hanged by the rope around his neck. The man lived during the Iron Age, a period dating from about 800BCE in Europe, when iron was the most important metal for weapons and tools.*

The remains of Tollund Man in the Silkeborg Museum, Denmark

WHY WAS HE PRESERVED?

Tollund Man was so well preserved because he was buried in a bog. Organic remains, such as hair, skin, leather and wood, usually decay in the soil because of the action of bacteria. Bacteria need oxygen to survive, and in a bog, layers of moss prevent oxygen reaching the lower layers. Also, bog water contains acid. This tans skin like leather, preserving it and turning it brown.

The body was found in Tollund Fen. In ancient times, the area was home to a hunting people, whose tools, treasure and corpses are sometimes found preserved in the bog.

TOLLUND MAN

Tollund Man has provided historians with some fascinating remains which have proved to be a rich source of information. He also enthralls the wider world. The body of this Iron Age man allows us to find out what life was like in times very different from our own.

The curled-up body of Tollund Man, as he was discovered in Tollund Fen

ASLEEP IN THE PEAT

Tollund Man was found 2m below the surface of the bog, on his side, with his arms and legs bent. He was naked except for a hide belt around his waist and a cap on his head. The cap, made from eight pieces of leather sewn together, was tied with laces under his chin. A plaited leather rope was around his neck. This was nearly 2m long and formed a noose that could be tightened behind his neck. Tollund Man had short hair and was clean shaven except for some stubble on his lip, cheeks and chin.

Tollund Man is considered to have the best-preserved head of any early man. Scientists conserved it by soaking it in baths containing formalin, acetic acid, alcohol, wax, paraffin and other preservatives.

THE SCIENTIFIC INVESTIGATION

Experts at the National Museum examined Tollund Man inside and out. From his teeth, they estimated that he was well over 20 years old when he died and that he had been hanged, probably by the noose found around his neck. They examined food remains in his stomach, which showed that his last meal had been a porridge of grains and seeds. Grains and seeds are planted in the ground to produce next season's crop. They are a symbol of fertility and growth. Tollund Man's death after eating porridge may have been a midwinter ritual to ensure the return of spring.

Ancient body in the ice

It was September 1991. Two hikers were walking in the Ötztal region of the Italian Alps. As they crossed a glacier, they spotted something dark in the ice up ahead. They went to investigate and discovered a human body sticking out of the glacier. Whose body was it and how did it come to be there?

EXAMINING THE BODY

When the two hikers found the body in the ice, they assumed it was the remains of a climber. They reported it to the police, and a helicopter was sent to retrieve the body. Several items lying on the ground nearby were also collected and taken with the body. When forensic scientists examined the corpse, they realized that it was very old. They called in Konrad Spindler (b.1939), a professor of archaeology at the University of Innsbruck. *Eureka!* He said the body was prehistoric and more than 4,000 years old.

> ## 'It was clear that we were dealing with a prehistoric find.'
>
> KONRAD SPINDLER
> *Professor of archaeology*

ÖTZI'S CLOTHING

Working with only tiny scraps of leather and bits of dried grass, scientists discovered that Ötzi was dressed warmly for life in the mountains. He wore a leather loincloth, fur leggings, a coat made of animal pelts, a cape made of woven grass and a bearskin hat tied under his chin. His leather shoes had plaited grass straps and were stuffed with grass for warmth.

Ötzi was carrying an unfinished bow about 2m long, and arrows in a deerskin quiver. He carried other items in a large leather rucksack.

ANCIENT EVIDENCE

The news of the discovery caused great excitement. A prehistoric man had been found with his original tools: a wooden bow, a flint dagger, a wooden axe with a copper blade and a pouch containing fire-lighting equipment. The scientists who examined him named him Ötzi after the region in the Alps where he was found. They established that he was 1.6m tall and had a brown beard and wavy brown hair. He was about 40 years old when he died.

Ötzi *was discovered by hikers in an Alpine glacier. He had been buried and preserved by centuries of snow, but as ice on the surface of the glacier melted the body was gradually exposed.*

RESEARCH CONTINUES

Since his discovery, Ötzi has been examined by more than 100 experts. One scientist who was X-raying him found a flint arrowhead in his shoulder. This suggests Ötzi died after an accident or fight. He has been on display in the South Tyrol Museum of Archaeology in Bolzano, Italy, close to the place where the body was discovered. But he has been deteriorating. Experts hope that his move to a special refrigerated 'igloo' in the museum, in December 2003, will prevent this.

ÖTZI THE ICEMAN

Ötzi is the oldest human mummy ever to have been preserved by freezing. His discovery opened a window on life towards the end of the Stone Age (about 2000BCE), a time in which farming spread and people began to settle in organized communities. Ötzi has been a huge attraction. Every year, thousands of tourists visit the museum at Bolzano to gaze at the prehistoric man.

A living fossil from the deep

S cientists in the 1930s knew all about the coelacanth (pronounced 'see-la-kanth'): it was a fish that had swum in ancient seas long before the age of the dinosaurs, and had died out about 80 million years ago. So imagine their amazement when, in 1938, a living specimen of one of these ancient fish was caught by fishermen in the sea off South Africa.

A coelacanth fossil. These fossils date back nearly 400 million years.

THE FOSSIL MYSTERY

Scientists learn about ancient creatures from the fossils they leave behind. The oldest coelacanth fossils have been found in rocks dating back more than 360 million years, but most of them date from about 240 million years ago, when coelacanth numbers were at their peak. Before the discovery in 1938, coelacanths were believed to have died out about 80 million years ago, because no later fossil had ever been found. How could the fish disappear for so long and then turn up alive and well? The answer seems to be that coelacanths changed their habitats from deep water to shallower water inside caves or under reefs close to newly formed volcanic islands. Here their remains broke up before they could turn into fossils.

A STRANGE FISH

Marjorie Courtenay-Latimer (b.1907) was the curator of a tiny museum in the port town of East London, South Africa. Captain Goosen (d.1988), a local fisherman, often invited her to inspect his catch and she took interesting specimens for the museum. On 23 December 1938, Courtenay-Latimer was standing on deck when she noticed a blue fin sticking out of a pile of rays and sharks. It was attached to a large fish, nearly 2m long. No one had any idea what it was, so Marjorie took it away to find out.

IDENTIFICATION

Courtenay-Latimer searched through her books and found a fish that seemed to match the one she had found. But it was prehistoric. She posted a sketch of her fish to Professor J L B Smith (d.1968), a fish biologist at a nearby university. On 3 January 1939, Courtenay-Latimer received a cable from Smith in which he told her to preserve the parts that would help him identify it. He hurried to East London. *Eureka!* He identified the fish as a 'prehistoric' coelacanth. It was like finding a living dinosaur.

Unlike most fish, whose tails have two sections called lobes, the **coelacanth's** *tail has three lobes. It was this that made the fish so easy for Smith to identify. Coelacanths from East Africa are blue, while Indonesian ones are brown.*

A SECOND FISH

A photo of Courtenay-Latimer and her fish was soon in newspapers around the world. Smith longed to find a second coelacanth so that he could study the internal organs. He posted notices up and down the East African coast, offering a reward. In December 1952, a fish was caught off the Comoros Islands, between Tanzania and the island of Madagascar. Smith was overjoyed. But his fish was more common than he had known. In 1998, coelacanths were found off Indonesia, 10,000km away.

Marjorie Courtenay-Latimer and her fish

Professor Smith *(holding fish) was photographed with the second fish. He later had it preserved.*

A living coelacanth in the Indian Ocean off East Africa

COELACANTH
Marjorie Courtenay-Latimer's discovery of the coelacanth made her an overnight celebrity, and thousands of people came to her museum to see the fish. The species was named Latimeria chalumnae *in her honour. It was the zoological find of the century, providing fascinating clues about evolution.*

'The most beautiful fish I had ever seen.'

MARJORIE COURTENAY-LATIMER
Museum curator

Wild horses of the Asian steppes

Thousands of years ago, wild horses roamed all over Europe and northern and Central Asia, grazing on the open grasslands. But about 10,000 years ago, their numbers began to dwindle, and at some time in the 18th century CE, they were believed to be extinct. So it was a great sensation when, in 1881, Russian explorer Colonel Nikolai Przewalski (1839–1888) discovered herds of wild horses in the grasslands of Central Asia.

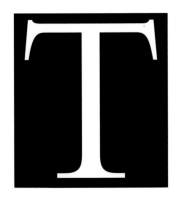

WILD HORSES
There are many different kinds of horse. Of all the breeds alive today, including those that live in the wild, all but one have descended from domesticated horses. The odd-horse-out is the 'wild horse of Asia'. Its DNA (the genetic code that passes on features to the next generation) is entirely different from that of other horses. This wild horse was believed to be extinct.

EXPLORING CENTRAL ASIA
In the late 19th century, the ruler of Russia, Tsar Alexander II (1818–1881), sent explorers through his vast empire on expeditions of discovery. One of these explorers, Colonel Przewalski (left), made several trips to Central Asia. Returning home from an expedition in 1879, he was given the skull and hide of a wild horse by the chief of a border control post. Przewalski was taken aback because he had thought wild horses were extinct. He took the remains to the St Petersburg university where a zoologist confirmed they were indeed the remains of a wild horse.

*This **prehistoric painting** of a horse is from the Lascaux caves in France (see pages 48–49), and was painted about 17,000 years ago. There are more horses in these paintings than any other animal, suggesting that the horses existed in huge numbers. They began to decline about 10,000 years ago, from hunting and the loss of their habitat due to a change in the earth's climate.*

Przewalski's horse *is aggressive, fast and almost impossible to tame.*

! PRZEWALSKI'S HORSE

Przewalski's discovery made him famous, and his name lives on in the species he found, which is known as Equus przewalskii. *The Russian explorer probably saved the wild horse from extinction. The news of his discovery alerted the world to the plight of the endangered horse. All of the wild horses alive today are descended from 12 that were caught in the wild in about 1900.*

RETURN TO MONGOLIA

Przewalski was determined to find the wild horses. In 1881, he returned to Central Asia, and in Mongolia he came across horses grazing near the Gobi Desert. They were not like any horse he had seen before. They were small, stocky and shy. *Eureka!* Przewalski had found wild horses. News of the discovery was greeted with amazement and spread across Russia to Europe. In order to save the horse, some foals were captured and taken to Europe for breeding. Today, there are about 1,200 of these horses living in captivity; small groups of them are being reintroduced to Mongolia.

Przewalski's horses grazing on the grasslands of Mongolia

THE WILD HORSE OF ASIA

Przewalski's horse is smaller than most domestic horses – about 1.2m high to the shoulders and 2m long. It is stockily built with a large head and bulging forehead. Like the zebra, it has an upright crest of short, stiff hairs on its head and neck. Its coat varies from dark brown around the mane to pale brown on the flanks and yellowing-white on the belly, with a dark stripe along its backbone.

Monsters on a South Sea island

For years, the world had heard strange rumours about an animal living on Komodo, a remote, rocky island in Indonesia. The creature, which had a reputation as a fearsome predator, was said to be a monster from the ancient past. Could these rumours possibly be true? In 1926, an American explorer set out on a long and dangerous journey to Komodo to find out.

The Komodo dragon, the largest lizard in the world

ALL ABOUT KOMODO DRAGONS

The Komodo dragon belongs to a group of giant lizards called monitors. It has short, powerful legs and long claws. From snout to tail, it measures about 3m and it weighs about 136kg. Komodo dragons find food by 'tasting' the air with their long, forked tongue. The animals are scavengers, but also hunters. They can bring down animals such as water buffalo, wild boar, goats and deer, which they kill by biting them and infecting them with their poisonous saliva.

AN AMERICAN ADVENTURER

W Douglas Burden (1898–1978) was a wealthy American hunter looking for adventure. With the backing of the American Museum of Natural History, he organized an expedition to find the mysterious 'dragons' of Komodo. He hoped to catch a pair and bring them back to New York. He set out on the 24,000km trip with a reptile expert, a big-game hunter and his young wife.

> 'He swung his grim head this way and that… a primeval monster in a primeval setting.'
>
> **W DOUGLAS BURDEN**
> *Adventurer*

ON TRACK

Not long after their arrival on the island, Burden spotted some gigantic footprints – just like fossilized dinosaur tracks he had seen in museums back home. He soon saw the animal that had made them. It was a huge lizard with a massive head and a forked tongue. *Eureka!* Burden had found the 'monster'!

Burden's expedition inspired the film **King Kong** *(1933), in which a giant creature is taken to New York.*

SUCCESS!

Burden returned to New York with two live Komodo dragons and 12 preserved ones. The live animals were taken to a zoo, and the preserved ones were given to the American Museum of Natural History. Komodo dragons still live on Komodo and a few other islands in Indonesia, but sadly their forest habitat is shrinking because trees are being cut down for timber and to make way for roads and farms. With only about 5,000 of these creatures alive today, they face an uncertain future.

KOMODO DRAGON

Reports of a living species of giant lizard had come as a complete surprise to experts. When Burden brought back Komodo dragons to New York, it proved the existence of the remarkable animals and caught the imagination of the public. The expedition was also a personal triumph for Burden.

A Komodo dragon *can burst out of a hiding place with terrifying speed.*

Earth's riches

Throughout history, there have been some
remarkable discoveries that have revealed the earth's
hidden treasures. Explorers, scientists, cowboys and an
empress have all found amazing things,
some by chance, some through dedicated
investigation. From the humble coffee bean to
glittering gemstones, these discoveries have
changed the course of people's lives and even
shaped the history of nations.

Riches in a California river

In 1848, a wealthy land developer called John Sutter (1803–1880) was building houses in northern California, USA. He needed a ready supply of timber and decided to construct a sawmill in the Sacramento hills. While the mill was under construction, the building manager, James Marshall (1810–1885), spotted some yellow metal glittering in a ditch. Could it be gold?

THE DISCOVERY

John Sutter was building his sawmill in Coloma, a small town on the banks of the American river. Each night, the river was diverted to run underneath the mill to form a deep ditch. Every morning the flow was stopped so that building work could continue. It was on 24 January 1848 that Sutter's builder and partner, James Marshall, saw some small shiny lumps of metal in the drained ditch. He decided to test one to see if it was gold, by smashing it between two rocks. The nugget flattened but did not shatter. *Eureka!* It was gold.

Miners in California *looked for gold by panning. They put gravel into shallow pans then carefully washed it out. Any gold was left behind in the pan because it was heavier than the gravel.*

GOLD
It turned out that the discovery of gold ruined John Sutter and James Marshall, but it had an important influence on the development of the American West. Many hundreds of thousands of fortune-seekers moved to California, which is still known as 'the golden state'.

SUTTER'S SECRET

Marshall showed Sutter the metal. The two men inspected the ditch the next few mornings and found more gold. They realized the hills must be full of it. Sutter asked his workers to keep the gold a secret until they had finished building the sawmill. But the lure of wealth was too great and, one by one, his workers left him to look for gold. Soon there was no one left working on Sutter's mill or in his business.

FROM RICHES TO RUIN

For Sutter, things went from bad to worse. The secret of the gold leaked out and people flocked to the area. They helped themselves to Sutter's land, and he could do nothing about it. Then the Gold Rush began in earnest. Tens of thousands of people headed to California to look for gold. Some people made fortunes overnight. Others made nothing at all. Marshall was awarded a small state pension in recognition of his discovery, but both he and Sutter died poor and bitter men. The search for gold lasted nearly 20 years, until the metal became too difficult to find. Today, tourists can visit a replica of Sutter's Mill at Coloma and see the spot where Marshall first spotted the gold in a ditch.

Gold is a precious metal with a beautiful colour and shine. It is soft and easy to work with and does not tarnish. For thousands of years, it has been used to make jewellery and other precious items. Shown here are a gold hair ornament set with diamonds, dating from about 1860 (left), and a lump of pure gold called a nugget (below).

'They got gold fever like everyone else.'

JOHN SUTTER
Land developer

THE GOLD RUSH

The Gold Rush began one of the largest human migrations in history. Half a million people from around the world endured long, dangerous journeys by land and sea to California. Arriving in 1849, the 'forty-niners', as the new immigrants were called, discovered a harsh reality. Life in the gold fields was lonely and dangerous, and mining was back-breaking work. Many of them found nothing, and those who made money often drank or gambled it away. Some miners became merchants instead, and earned a fortune selling goods and services for wildly inflated prices.

A replica of Sutter's Mill, part of the James Marshall Gold Discovery State Historic Park at Coloma, California

A secret world underground

In 1901, a 19-year-old cowboy called Jim White was working near the town of Carlsbad in the mountains of New Mexico, USA. One evening, he saw a strange black cloud emerging from the ground. It turned out to be millions of bats flying out of a hole. Where could they be coming from? White decided to explore.

In the summer, Carlsbad Caverns are home to seven species of bat, including the **Mexican freetail bat** *(right). During the day, about 5 million bats sleep in the caverns. In the evening, they all stream out.*

THE BATS' HOME

Jim White returned to the hole in the ground with a lamp, some rope and wire. He made a simple ladder and climbed down it into the hole. He soon found himself 45m below, standing in piles of bats' droppings. He climbed through an opening in the rock. *Eureka!* White entered an enormous cavern with huge stalagmites rising from the floor and stalactites hanging from the ceiling. It was a breathtaking sight!

THE GUANO MINE

White returned to explore the caverns many times. He found passageways and chambers, some large enough to hold a cathedral. He told people about his find but no one really believed him. Then a Carlsbad merchant bought the mining rights to the caverns: the bat droppings, called guano, would make valuable fertilizer. He drilled a shaft into a cavern and rigged up a steel bucket to collect the guano.

On summer evenings, visitors wait to watch swarms of bats leaving the caverns to feed

HOW THE CAVERNS WERE FORMED

The Carlsbad Caverns National Park contains about 100 caverns with high, vaulted ceilings and amazing rock formations. Geologists believe that the limestone caverns first formed more than 200 million years ago, when an undersea reef was raised above sea level and was then hollowed out by seeping groundwater. When the groundwater later fell, the hollows in the rock filled with air. Finally, over thousands of years, dripping rainwater deposited minerals, which built the formations that can be seen today.

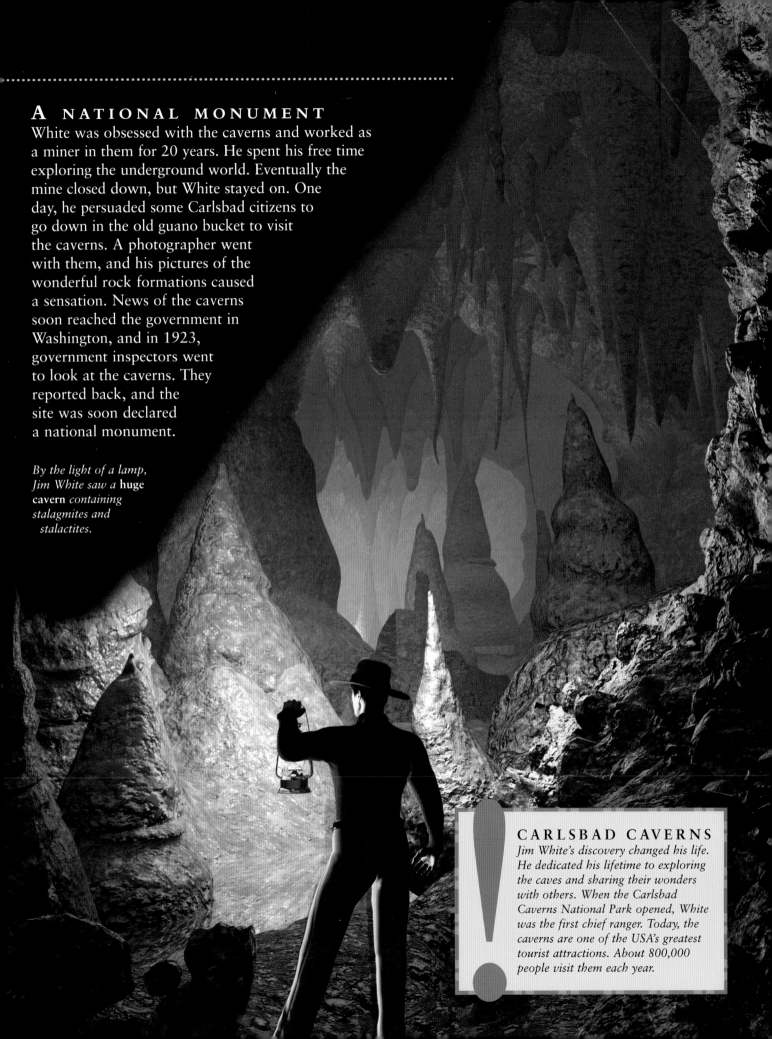

A NATIONAL MONUMENT

White was obsessed with the caverns and worked as a miner in them for 20 years. He spent his free time exploring the underground world. Eventually the mine closed down, but White stayed on. One day, he persuaded some Carlsbad citizens to go down in the old guano bucket to visit the caverns. A photographer went with them, and his pictures of the wonderful rock formations caused a sensation. News of the caverns soon reached the government in Washington, and in 1923, government inspectors went to look at the caverns. They reported back, and the site was soon declared a national monument.

By the light of a lamp, Jim White saw a **huge cavern** *containing stalagmites and stalactites.*

CARLSBAD CAVERNS
Jim White's discovery changed his life. He dedicated his lifetime to exploring the caves and sharing their wonders with others. When the Carlsbad Caverns National Park opened, White was the first chief ranger. Today, the caverns are one of the USA's greatest tourist attractions. About 800,000 people visit them each year.

Hot spots on the ocean floor

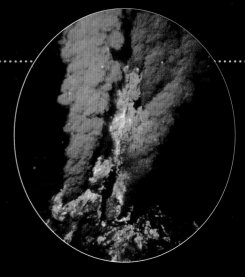

D eep-sea vents are cracks in the earth's crust where hot water gushes up through the seabed. In the 1960s, scientists studying the chemistry of the oceans predicted the vents existed, but no one had ever found one. In 1977, explorer Robert Ballard (b. 1942) was determined to do so.

On a later expedition, Ballard found vents now known as **black smokers**. *The 'smoke' is hot water that looks dark because it is full of dissolved materials. These settle around the vent and build a chimney-like structure many metres tall.*

WAITING FOR A SIGN

On board a ship near the Galapagos Islands in the Pacific Ocean, Robert Ballard and a team of scientists were looking for signs of a deep-sea vent. They were towing a steel cage named *Angus* along the ocean floor. *Angus* had lights, a camera and temperature sensors, which would detect warm water. One night, *Angus* sent out a signal. It had found a hot spot!

FINDING A VENT

The next morning, three scientists climbed into a submersible called *Alvin* and dived down more than 2km to the hot spot. They saw warm, shimmering water bubbling up through cracks in the seabed. *Eureka!* They had found a deep-sea vent. The hot water turned cloudy as it mixed with the sea, and materials that had been dissolved in it stained the seabed brown.

A spider crab picks its way over small tube worms on the seabed near a deep-sea vent

LIFE AROUND THE VENTS

The area around deep-sea vents teems with white crabs, huge tube worms, giant clams, shrimps and many other creatures. For most of the time, this undersea community survives in icy darkness, but occasionally it is blasted by boiling water and sometimes destroyed by flows of molten rock. In some places, bright red tube worms grow up to 2m long (see main picture, right). They live inside tubes of horny material, which protect them from predators such as crabs.

WHAT CAUSES THE VENTS?

Deep-sea hydrothermal vents are deep cracks in the seabed, caused by movements of the earth's crust. Seawater seeps down through the cracks and is heated by molten rock inside the earth. The hot water later gushes out of the vents, carrying gases and dissolved materials from deep inside the earth.

A SURPRISING DISCOVERY

The scientists in *Alvin* made another discovery that came as a complete surprise: there were hundreds of clams and other animals living around the vents. Finding life in this dark place, where water gushed out at ferocious temperatures, was extraordinary. What could the animals be feeding on? *Eureka!* It was bacteria, feeding on the gases and materials pouring out of the vents. Before this discovery, it was thought that all energy for life came from the sun. But the energy for this life was coming from deep inside the earth.

Scientists saw the amazing community of animals from the submersible **Alvin**. *This high-tech mini-submarine is just 7m long and can carry a pilot and two scientists as deep as 4,500m. It has lights, video cameras and robotic arms to take samples from the seabed.*

DEEP-SEA VENTS

The discovery of deep-sea vents was one of the most important oceanographic discoveries of the 20th century. It showed that some animals were supported by energy from inside the earth. This changed our view of life and helped to explain the chemistry of the oceans.

Fuel for a new age

People always knew there was oil in Texas, USA. For centuries, it had been seeping out of the ground but no one tried to drill for it until the late 1800s. The first oil wells produced so little that they were shut down. But one geologist was sure there was more oil and he was determined to find it!

THE SEARCH FOR OIL

American geologist Patillo Higgins (1863–1955) believed there was oil under a small hill known as Spindletop, near the town of Beaumont in Texas. Locals thought Higgins's ideas were nonsense, but he hired an engineer called Anthony Lucas (1855–1921) who began drilling in the area. After a while, Higgins ran out of money and he pulled out of the enterprise. But Lucas wanted to keep trying, so he formed a new company with a team of oilmen. They surveyed the area, picked a spot and began drilling in October 1900. By Christmas, they had found nothing and stopped for the holiday.

On the morning of 10 January 1901, oil gushed out of a hole in the ground on a hill called Spindletop, near Beaumont, Texas. The greenish-black oil 'gusher' measured about 15cm across, and rose to a height of more than 50m, doubling the size of the drilling derrick (right). It was more oil than had ever been seen anywhere in the world.

OIL AT SPINDLETOP
The discovery of oil reserves at Spindletop opened people's eyes to the potential of the fuel. New machines like cars and planes were invented, which sparked an industrial revolution in the USA and led to an economic boom.

THE GUSHER

Work began again in the New Year, and the drillers had soon reached a depth of 300m. Then, on the morning of 10 January 1901, something remarkable happened. As drillers lowered the drill into the hole, mud bubbled up to the surface and the drill shot out of the ground. A short silence followed and then, with a noise like cannon shot, something black gushed out of the hole. *Eureka!* It was oil.

THE OIL AGE

Lucas had hoped to find a well that would produce five barrels of oil a day. (A barrel is 159 litres.) In fact, the well at Spindletop produced nearly 100,000 barrels a day – more than all the other oil wells in the USA combined! Oil is still big in Texas. It is the second-largest oil-producing state in the USA, after Alaska, and provides the raw material for the huge petrochemical industry in the wealthy city of Houston.

A crew stands by to mend an oil well at Beaumont, Texas

THE OIL BOOM

Following the discovery of oil, the population at Beaumont grew from 10,000 to 50,000 almost overnight. Production ran wild with nearly 300 wells fighting for space on top of Spindletop hill. Swindlers then moved in, persuading people to invest in hoax oil companies that never made any money. Soon Spindletop became known as 'Swindletop'.

The discovery of vast reserves of oil led to the invention of the **motor car**, *fuelling America's manufacturing industry.*

A fortune in the ground

In 1866, Hopetown was just a tiny village in the British Cape Colony in southern Africa. One day, a young Hopetown farmer, Schalk van Niekerk (c.1824–1880), was visiting a neighbour when he saw the neighbour's teenage son playing with a shiny white pebble. Van Niekerk was interested in unusual stones, and something about this pebble caught his eye. He persuaded his neighbours to let him take the pebble home and find out more about it.

*This **1950s necklace** contains more than 100 diamonds, including a pear-shaped, 67-carat gem from South Africa. Diamonds form deep inside the earth over millions of years. The stones are cut and polished into many-sided gems that catch and reflect the light.*

THE GLITTERING PEBBLE

Van Niekerk showed the stone to a local trader, who sent it to an expert. *Eureka!* It was a 21-carat diamond. (A carat equals 0.2g.) It was bought by the Governor of the Cape Colony for £500. Later, it became known as the Eureka because it was the first diamond found in South Africa.

DIAMOND RUSH

Hopetown boomed in the diamond rush. Miners bought claims to small plots of land, put up their tents and began to dig. Later, when miners moved to Kimberley, Hopetown became an important supply centre and its farmers were paid huge prices to transport goods north. Wild spending sprees took place in the town: men lit cigars with banknotes and women bathed in champagne! But the boom and the excitement did not last: when a new railway bypassed Hopetown on its way to the Kimberley Mine, the town was soon forgotten.

Diamond mining *was dangerous work, and the European settlers' greed for diamonds led to abuse of African workers.*

DIAMONDS AT KIMBERLEY

The discovery of diamonds in southern Africa had a huge impact on the region. Large companies bought out the small miners and took control of the mines. The diamonds generated great wealth, although not for the African population, and boosted the area's economy.

A SECOND FIND

Everyone thought the Eureka was a fluke. They said the stone must have been dropped by an ostrich – a bird that swallows stones to digest its food. But two years later, a local witch doctor found a similar, larger stone in the same area. He took it to Schalk van Niekerk, who exchanged it for 500 sheep, ten oxen and a horse. The stone was found to be an 83-carat diamond, later named the Star of South Africa.

> 'This is the rock on which the future success of South Africa will be built.'
>
> **RICHARD SOUTHEY**
> *Colonial Secretary at the Cape (1834–1899)*

*The Kimberley Mine became known as **the Big Hole** and now forms part of an open-air museum. The Eureka diamond is also on display at the museum.*

DIAMOND FEVER

Tens of thousands of treasure hunters rushed to Hopetown in the Northern Cape with the dream of finding their own diamonds. The Diamond Rush had begun! The hopeful miners moved from place to place, following each new find. Finally, they settled about 100km north of Hopetown, in an area that became known as Kimberley. This was the start of southern Africa's diamond industry, and today this region is still one of the biggest diamond producers in the world.

The mighty secret of Africa

A bout 150 years ago, much of Africa had not been explored by Europeans. Geographers longed to discover its secrets, especially the source of the River Nile. In 1856, the Royal Geographical Society in London sent an expedition to find it.

THE EXPEDITION

Richard Burton (1821–1890) and John Hanning Speke (1827–1864) led the expedition. They landed on Africa's eastern coast in June 1857 and set off west through what is now Tanzania. Five months and 960km later, they reached a place called Tabora. Here they were told about a huge lake to the west, so they went to explore it. They found the lake (Lake Tanganyika), but no river flowing north. By now it was May 1858 and their health was bad. They returned to Tabora to rest.

The River Nile is the world's longest river. It flows north out of Lake Victoria in Uganda to the Mediterranean Sea. The Ripon Falls, which Speke identified as the river's source, were submerged in 1954 following the construction of the Owen Falls dam.

SOURCE OF THE NILE

John Hanning Speke's discovery of the main source of the Nile solved one of the mysteries of 19th-century geography. But Speke was slipshod in his methods and he could not provide solid proof about the source of the Nile. It was not until 1875 that the explorer and journalist Henry Morton Stanley (1841–1904) proved beyond doubt that Speke was right.

*Author, explorer, scientist and poet, Richard Burton was a remarkable personality with a fiery temper. He was a brilliant linguist and spoke more than 30 languages. He loved Arab cultures and often wore Eastern clothes, such as this **hat and shoes**.*

Burton's flat-topped Muslim hat, known as a fez

Eastern slippers with curling toes, worn by Burton

John Hanning Speke *was an ex-Indian Army man. After completing ten years' service, he planned to explore Africa, gathering specimens of rare birds and other animals. Instead, he joined Burton's expedition. Puritanical and brooding, he was the opposite of the eccentric Burton.*

SPEKE'S DISCOVERY

Back in Tabora, the expedition heard about another huge lake, this time to the north. Unfortunately, Burton was too ill to move, so Speke set out to investigate on his own. In August 1858, he found and named the enormous Lake Victoria, which he was convinced was the source of the Nile. Speke returned to Burton with the news of his discovery but Burton thought that Speke was wrong, and the two men quarrelled. Exhausted, they decided to return to Britain.

THE SOURCE IS FOUND

Speke arrived in London ahead of Burton and reported to the Royal Geographical Society. By the time Burton arrived, Speke had been commissioned to lead a new expedition to settle the Nile question once and for all. Speke set out in 1860. In July 1862, he found and named the Ripon Falls to the north of Lake Victoria. *Eureka!* He had found the source of the mighty River Nile at last.

END OF A FRIENDSHIP

Burton and Speke were on a collision course before they returned home. They had agreed to talk together to the press, but before Burton arrived in Britain, Speke had announced that he thought Lake Victoria was the source of the Nile. After Speke's second expedition, Burton still thought he was wrong, but the day before they were due to have a public debate about the issue, Speke died in a shooting accident.

Speke (standing left) presents his case to a meeting of the Royal Geographical Society. Burton is standing right.

Coffea arabica
The coffee plant

Berries for a special drink

In the 10th century CE, according to legend, a goatherd named Kaldi was grazing his goats in the Ethiopian mountains. One night, he noticed them behaving rather oddly. Instead of sleeping soundly as usual, they were wide awake and jumping around. The goatherd decided to investigate, and he discovered something that would become popular all over the world.

COFFEE CULTIVATION

Coffee is such a popular drink that it is now cultivated on farms and plantations in more than 50 countries. The plant will grow only in tropical regions, where the weather is always warm. After flowering, the berries, known as cherries, form on the plant. These change colour as they ripen, from green to yellow and finally to red. Inside each cherry are two green beans, which turn brown when they are roasted. These are then ground and mixed with hot water to make the drink. Each plant produces about 2,000 cherries in a growing season, enough to make 500g of roasted coffee.

Harvesting coffee in Costa Rica

FRISKY GOATS

When Kaldi the goatherd took his goats into the mountains, he knew they would find enough to eat. They could survive in much more difficult conditions. When they did not go to sleep as usual, Kaldi remembered he had seen them eating berries from some small bushes, and he went to look at the plants. They had glossy leaves, white flowers and clusters of hard berries the size and colour of cherries. Kaldi tasted the berries and soon felt invigorated and more awake. *Eureka!* He had discovered the effect of coffee.

STRANGE BREW

Not long after, a Muslim monk passed by, and Kaldi told him about the berries he had found. The monk picked some and took them to his monastery. There, he crushed them and mixed them with hot water. He found that when he drank some of the bitter-tasting brew, it helped him to stay awake during long hours of prayer. He and his fellow monks began to supply other monasteries with the 'Kaffa' berries, which were named after the region in Ethiopia where they were found. The 'Kaffa' drink was soon in great demand.

The world's first coffee shop opened in 1475 in Constantinople, Turkey. Soon coffee was so popular that it was banned by the ruling sultan. The ban had little effect and coffee drinking boomed.

COFFEE
The discovery of coffee brought a completely new drink to the world. Coffee was also used in some countries as a medicine. The impact of the drink was small at first, but over hundreds of years, its popularity spread across the world. Today, about 400 billion cups are enjoyed worldwide every year.

'Black as the devil, hot as hell, pure as an angel, sweet as love.'

CHARLES MAURICE DE TALLEYRAND
(French statesman 18th–19th century)

An 18th-century CE engraving of 'a Turkish girl taking coffee on a sofa'

COFFEE TRAVELS

Coffee travelled with traders from Africa over the Red Sea to Arabia and on to Turkey. There, people used just the beans inside the berries. They roasted them, ground them and boiled them in water. In the early 1600s, coffee reached Europe. Pope Clement VIII (pope 1592–1605) liked it so much that he baptized it and gave it his approval. Gradually, a craze spread through Europe and later to the USA. Coffee houses sprang up where people could meet and talk about the news of the day. Today, coffee is still a social drink – and a global industry.

Luxury in ancient China

A bout 4,700 years ago, Emperor Huang-Ti of China (c.2704–2598BCE) had a fine garden. He was very proud of it but he was worried because something was damaging his mulberry trees. He asked his wife, Hsi-Ling-Shi, to find out what it was. What she found became worth its weight in gold.

Farmed silkworms spinning cocoons

HOW SILK IS MADE

Silk is a fine cloth woven from the threads of the silkworm. This tiny creature, the caterpillar of the *Bombyx* moth, spins a cocoon from a long sticky thread before changing into an adult. When several threads are spun together, they form a strong glossy yarn that can be woven into silk. Today, most silk comes from small farms in China and the Far East, where it is an important 'green' industry. It does not cause waste or pollution, and its raw materials are renewable resources.

THE EMPEROR'S GARDEN

Hsi-Ling-Shi was only 14 when, according to legend, she went to inspect her husband's mulberry trees. She discovered that white caterpillars were eating the leaves and then spinning shiny cocoons around themselves. Hsi-Ling-Shi tried to kill the caterpillars in hot water, but as she put a cocoon in the water, she noticed it unravelling into a long thread.

WEAVING SILK

The empress was intrigued by the thread. She twisted it into a yarn, which she then wove into cloth. The material was smooth and shimmered in the light. *Eureka!* She had discovered silk. Soon she had her own mulberry trees and looms on which her servants wove lengths of cloth. When the silk was dyed, it shone with jewel-rich colours and made handsome gifts for visitors to the emperor's court.

This rare Chinese silk robe dates from the time of the emperor Qianlong (ruled CE1736–1795). It is richly embroidered with a pattern of dragons.

This **terracotta camel,** *dating from* CE618–907, *is loaded with silk. Trade flourished along the Silk Road, with traders carrying cloth, spices, jade and other goods from China to the Mediterranean Sea.*

THE SECRET OF SILK

In time, silk was taken to the West along a trade route known as the Silk Road. Everywhere, its luxury was greatly admired. For the next 3,000 years, the Chinese kept the manufacture of silk a closely guarded secret. Eventually, in about CE550, the Roman emperor Justinian (CE482–565) sent two spies to China. They smuggled silk moth eggs and mulberry seeds inside their walking sticks, and China's great secret was out at last.

SILK

The discovery of silk brought great wealth to ancient China. The appetite for silk in the West encouraged trading links between Rome and China, and the Silk Road, a 4,000km-long trade route, developed. Traders carried news and customs, so ideas were exchanged between East and West.

Lost wonders

Every year, thousands of tourists marvel at the terracotta army of a Chinese emperor, the Inca city of Machu Picchu, and the prehistoric cave paintings at Lascaux in France. They are famous today, but many of the world's greatest historical treasures were shrouded in mystery for hundreds or thousands of years. Some were known only to local people until explorers stumbled upon them or sought them out and opened them up to the wider world. Others were hidden completely, buried in the ground, under the sea or walled up in secret caves. Their discovery has helped us to uncover a wealth of information about human history – about the rise and fall of great civilizations and the lives of ordinary people and famous rulers.

A hidden city in the Andes

Between the 12th and 16th centuries CE, the great Inca civilization flourished high in the Andes mountains of Peru in South America. In 1532, Spanish adventurers known as *conquistadores* (conquerors) invaded the region and ransacked many of the Inca cities in search of gold. The Incas abandoned their other cities, which fell into ruin. One of these cities was Machu Picchu.

THE PROFESSOR

Hiram Bingham (1875–1956), professor of history at Yale University in the USA, had studied South American history for many years. In 1911, during a visit to Lima, Peru, he came across an old book that told of the fall of the Incas. He was inspired by the description of the Inca retreat and the ancient mountain cities they abandoned. Bingham decided to try to find the ancient Inca capital city.

> 'I know of no place in the world which can compare with it.'
>
> **HIRAM BINGHAM**
> *History professor*

MACHU PICCHU

Hiram Bingham's discovery of Machu Picchu made him world-famous. Years later, he was the inspiration for the fictional film hero, Indiana Jones. Arguably the greatest archaeological site in the Americas, Machu Picchu reveals fascinating facts about Inca civilization and encourages many thousands to visit Peru.

Machu Picchu stands on a remote ridge in the Andes mountains, about 2,500m above sea level. The town, overlooked by towering peaks, was abandoned by its Inca inhabitants. Amazingly, the Spanish never found it during the 300 years that Peru was part of the Spanish Empire.

A NERVE-WRACKING CLIMB

Bingham mounted an expedition. He and his party went to Cusco in the foothills of the Andes. From there, they climbed into the Urubamba gorge. On 23 July 1911, the group camped on the land of a local farmer, who told Bingham about ruins on top of a ridge. Bingham paid the farmer to guide him there and the two set out one cold, drizzly morning. It was a nerve-wracking climb up steep, rocky slopes and along narrow mountain paths. At times, the professor had to crawl on his hands and knees across narrow bridges spanning terrifying gorges and ravines.

A SENSATIONAL FIND

At the top of the ridge, Bingham and the farmer rested in a hut, where locals told them about the nearby ruins. An 11-year-old boy then escorted the professor past overgrown terraces to some white granite walls. Bingham saw palaces, temples, terraces and towers. *Eureka!* It was an ancient Inca city, known to locals as Machu Picchu. Bingham was overwhelmed. He led three further expeditions to Machu Picchu during the next four years.

Shaped granite blocks in the Royal Tomb of Machu Picchu beneath the Temple of the Sun

BUILDING MACHU PICCHU

Built in 1450, Machu Picchu, which means 'old mountain', is a spectacular, highly ordered city covering a site of about 8km². Its houses, temples, workshops and other buildings were built on simple lines. Large granite blocks were shaped and sanded by hand until they fitted together perfectly without the need for mortar. There were no rounded arches or decorative carvings. Beyond the city, the steep hillsides were terraced for farming, and fertile soil was brought up from the valley to grow sweet potatoes, sugar cane, yucca and corn.

A broken palace on the seabed

O n 14 April 1912, the liner *Titanic*, on its maiden voyage, struck an iceberg in the North Atlantic. It sank, and more than 1,500 passengers died. Over the next 70 years, many people tried to locate the wreck, but it was like looking for a needle in a haystack. Then, in September 1985, Robert Ballard (b. 1942) found the *Titanic*'s grave.

*These **fine silver objects** from the* Titanic's *dining rooms are some of the 6,000 or more objects that have been recovered from the seabed around the wreck. Other items include china and porcelain, toiletries and clothing, postcards and letters, newspapers and the ship's bell. These have been conserved by a team of experts, and many are now part of a touring exhibition to museums around the world.*

WHO IS ROBERT BALLARD?

Robert Ballard is an American geologist, marine scientist and ocean explorer. He has taken part in many expeditions to explore the seabed and its ancient wrecks. He was enthralled by the story of the *Titanic* and was sure that, with the right team and high-tech gear, he could find the wreck. In 1985, he and a group of American and French scientists began the quest. They planned to search the seabed in the area of *Titanic's* last reported position, then follow the course that any debris from the ship would have drifted on that fateful night.

Many wealthy people were tempted to sail on the Titanic's *maiden voyage. The ship symbolized style, glamour and luxury. It was no surprise that manufacturers used the liner's prestige to advertise their goods. In this poster, a soap company boasts that its luxury soap has been chosen for the first class passenger cabins.*

LUXURY TO DIE FOR

The *Titanic* was the largest vessel of its time. It was a floating palace rivalling the very best hotels on land. Crafted using only the finest materials, the liner offered top-of-the-range first, second and third class cabins. It also contained elegant public rooms, a grand stairway, a Parisian-style café, a Turkish bath, a gymnasium and squash courts. A one-way passage in a first class suite cost at least £500, the equivalent of a working person's wages for a whole year.

FIRST SIGHTING

Ballard and the French
co-leader, Jean-Louis Michel
(b. 1945), scoured the ocean
floor. They used the latest
sonar equipment and a
deep-sea video camera called
Argo. But all they saw was
mud and sand. Then, when
only five days of the expedition
remained, pipes, deck fittings
and a huge boiler appeared on
the video screen. Michel grabbed
the *Titanic's* construction records
and found the picture of its boiler.
It exactly matched the boiler on the
screen. *Eureka!* They had found
the long-lost wreck.

*The wreck of the Titanic was discovered
598km southeast of Newfoundland, Canada,
and 4km beneath the surface of the ocean. As
it sank, the ship broke into two huge pieces,
which now lie 610m apart.*

MOVING PICTURES

Over the next four days, *Argo* explored
the wreck more closely. But then the
expedition's time was up and Ballard
had to leave the site. The wreck's
location was kept a closely guarded
secret. The next summer, Ballard
returned to the *Titanic*, diving
down in the submersible *Alvin*.
Using a small robot that could get
inside the wreck, he recorded moving,
rather eerie pictures of the grand
staircase and other elegant fitments.
Ballard never forgot that the *Titanic*
was a grave, and when his expedition
ended, he left behind a plaque that
read: 'In memory of those souls
who perished with the *Titanic*
April 14/15, 1912'.

Ancient pictures in a hidden cave

In September 1940, four boys were walking in the grounds of Lascaux, an old manor house in southwest France. When their dog fell through a crack in some rocks, the boys went to rescue it and found that the hole led to a cavern. It would prove to be one of the most exciting archaeological discoveries of the 20th century.

A painting of cattle on the cave walls at Lascaux

CAVE ART

The artists who painted the pictures at Lascaux drew animals that were important to them. They may have thought the paintings would help them in their hunting. It must have been difficult to work in the dark, remote caves. The artists would have needed torches to see by and ladders to reach the high ceilings. The paints they used were made from natural pigments, plant roots, charcoal and sap, and dabbed on with fingers, sticks or pads of moss or fur.

The Lascaux caves are covered inside with pictures – some painted, others engraved or drawn. The pictures were made about 17,000 years ago during the early Stone Age, when people had not yet discovered metals and were using stone for tools.

FINDING THE CAVE

The four teenage boys who discovered the cavern were Marcel Ravidat, Jacques Marsal, Georges Agnel and Simon Coencas. The next day they returned to explore. They brought ropes, ladders and lights with them and lowered themselves down through the hole. Their eyes gradually adjusted to the darkness. *Eureka!* They saw that the walls of the cavern were covered in pictures. They could make out images of horses, deer and other animals. The boys knew they had made an amazing discovery.

CAVE PAINTINGS AT LASCAUX

The caves at Lascaux were one of the great archaeological discoveries of the 20th century. The paintings of prehistoric animals captured the world's imagination. They offer us a glimpse of the lives of our ancestors in the distant past.

A group of tourists visit the replica cave

THE FIRST VISITORS

News of the discovery travelled fast. People were soon flocking to explore the caves. In all, they found seven underground chambers connected by narrow passageways, with paintings and engravings on the ceilings and walls. A team of top archaeologists soon arrived at the caves. They were amazed by the sensational find: the paintings dated from about 15000BCE and were perfectly preserved. Archaeologists were worried about what to do with the caves. Europe was at war so there was no spare money to spend on developing and protecting the site. They decided to seal it up until after the war.

VISITS TO THE CAVE

The caves were opened to the public in 1948 and thousands of people visited them. But it soon became clear that the visitors were having a harmful effect. The gases and water vapour in their breath dampened the cave walls and damaged the precious paintings. Attempts were made to protect them, but in 1963, it was decided to close the caves. Twenty years later, a lifesize replica of the biggest cave was opened nearby.

Secrets of an ancient script

T he monuments and tombs of ancient Egypt are inscribed with a form of picture-writing known as hieroglyphs. For centuries, people had puzzled over these mysterious symbols, trying to decipher them. Then, in 1799, a stone slab was found by chance in the Egyptian desert. It became one of the most famous discoveries of ancient Egypt.

FINDING THE STONE

In the late 1790s, Emperor Napoleon Bonaparte (1769–1821) and the French army had invaded Egypt. In 1799, soldiers began to dig the foundations of a fort in the town of Rashid (known in English as Rosetta), on the Nile delta. As they dug in the sand, one of them came across a slab of black stone.

LANGUAGES AND SCRIPTS

One side of the stone was covered with an inscription. It was a decree issued in 196 BCE by Egyptian priests supporting Ptolemy V (c.210–180 BCE), the new Greek-born king of Egypt. The decree itself was not very interesting, but the way it was written was. The same piece of text had been inscribed three times: in Greek, Egyptian hieroglyphs and demotic script – a later, faster form of hieroglyphs. In 1801, Britain took control of Egypt, and the Rosetta Stone was packed up and sent to London. Historians at the British Museum hoped the inscription would help cryptographers (people who work out how to read codes) to decipher hieroglyphs. Their efforts were in vain.

*The first section of the **Rosetta Stone** is in hieroglyphs, the central section is in Egyptian demotic and the last section is in Greek. A search was made for the broken-off corners, but they were never found.*

THE ROSETTA STONE

The Rosetta Stone is the key that unlocked the secrets of ancient Egyptian hieroglyphs. For Jean-François Champollion, the interpretation of the picture symbols fulfilled a lifelong ambition. He had been obsessed with hieroglyphs since the age of ten and was determined to decipher them. His achievement opened up the entire written history of ancient Egypt.

People flocked to the British Museum to see the Rosetta Stone

A FORGOTTEN SCRIPT

Dating back over 5,000 years, hieroglyphs were used by the ancient Egyptians in state and ceremonial documents and on the walls of monuments and tombs. But the 700 picture symbols were too fussy for day-to-day use, so a faster form of writing evolved. This was called demotic script. Towards the end of the 4th century CE, hieroglyphs were banned by the Christian Church because they were thought to be pagan. Soon there was no one left who could understand them, and the script was forgotten until Champollion translated it about 1,400 years later.

*These **hieroglyphs** are from the tomb of Horemheb, king of Egypt (ruled 1348–1320BCE). The two ovals are cartouches containing hieroglyphs that make up a royal name. It was by looking at cartouches like these that Champollion deciphered hieroglyphs.*

DECIPHERING THE STONE

Twenty years later, a French linguist, Jean-François Champollion (1790–1832), got to work on the stone. Champollion had a good knowledge of ancient languages. Using Greek and Coptic, a language descended from ancient Egyptian, Champollion was able to identify the hieroglyphic characters of the name Ptolomys (Ptolemy). They were inscribed inside an oval called a cartouche, used for the names of rulers. Champollion then used the P, L and O to unravel another cartouche – this time for Kliopadra (Cleopatra). *Eureka!* Although there was still much work to do, Champollion had cracked the code!

'The most important event of the second millennium'

GRAHAM GREEN
Chairman of the Trustees of the British Museum 1996–2002

Ancient tomb of a boy king

In the desert to the west of Egypt's River Nile lies the Valley of the Kings. About 3,000 years ago, the rulers of Egypt, called pharaohs, chose to be buried there. By the early 20th century CE, about 60 of their tombs had been discovered, but the treasure that once surrounded the dead kings had long since disappeared. In 1922, the British archaeologist Howard Carter (1874–1939) found the unspoilt tomb of an Egyptian pharaoh. It belonged to the boy-king Tutankhamun (ruled c.1333–1324BCE).

THE ARCHAEOLOGIST

Howard Carter had visited Egypt several times from the age of 17, copying tomb paintings and inscriptions for Egyptian archaeologists. He started doing his own excavations and was convinced that Tutankhamun's tomb lay in the Valley of the Kings. In 1914, he began an excavation, sponsored by Lord Caernarvon (1866–1923), a wealthy British aristocrat.

THE HIDDEN STEPS

For years, Carter had no luck, but on 4 November 1922, his team uncovered stone steps leading to a sealed doorway. Carter noticed that the seals were inscribed with the name Nebkheprure, one of the names used by Tutankhamun. *Eureka!* Could this be the long-lost tomb? Carter dispatched a telegram to Lord Caernarvon and waited for his arrival.

'At last have made wonderful discovery.'

HOWARD CARTER
Archaeologist

THE EXCAVATION

The excavation of Tutankhamun's tomb took Carter ten long years. He worked methodically, numbering, sketching, photographing and measuring every object in the tomb's four rooms. Larger items had to be taken to pieces, and protection from the dry desert air was a priority. At last the treasures were transported to Cairo and put on display. Later, in the 1960s and 70s, they were exhibited around the world. Today the treasure is back in Cairo and Tutankhamun's mummified remains have returned to the Valley of the Kings.

This was the sight that met Carter's eyes when he first peered inside the tomb

THE GLINT OF GOLD

Nineteen days later, Caernarvon stood by Carter as he opened the doorway. Behind it lay a passage that led to another door. Carter made a hole in this doorway, lit a candle and peered through. As he later wrote, he saw 'strange animals, statues and gold – everywhere the glint of gold'. Behind the door was a small chamber crammed with furniture, chariots, weapons, jewellery – everything the pharaoh would need in the afterlife. It was an Egyptian treasure trove.

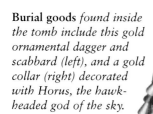

Burial goods *found inside the tomb include this gold ornamental dagger and scabbard (left), and a gold collar (right) decorated with Horus, the hawk-headed god of the sky.*

TUTANKHAMUN'S TOMB

Carter was about to give up his search for Tutankhamun's tomb when the steps were found. The discovery exceeded his wildest dreams: it was the first tomb of an Egyptian pharaoh to be found intact. His discovery created a huge interest in Egyptology.

Tutankhamun's mummy was found inside this **coffin case** *made of solid gold. The two tiny mummies of his stillborn children were also found nearby.*

Ancient scrolls in a desert cave

I n January 1947, a young Bedouin, Muhammed Adh-Dhib, was minding his goats in Qumran, Israel, on the northwest shore of the Dead Sea. It was evening, and realizing that one of his goats was missing, Adh-Dhib started to search for it among the rocks. Idly, he threw a stone into a cave and heard pottery breaking. He decided to return the next day to find out what it was. Adh-Dhib was about to make a sensational find.

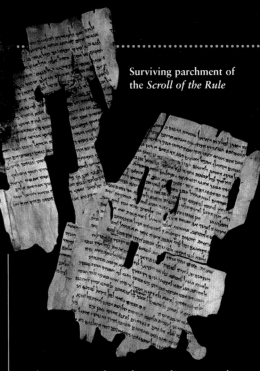

Surviving parchment of the Scroll of the Rule

These pieces of parchment, known as the **Scroll of the Rule,** *have been pieced together by scholars. The text sets out the rules of the Essenes' religious life and the punishments for those who broke them.*

JARS IN A CAVE

When Muhammed Adh-Dhib searched the cave in Qumran, he found seven old pottery jars. He lifted the lids, peered inside and pulled out some ancient scrolls wrapped in linen. Adh-Dhib took the scrolls and sold them to a Bethlehem antiques dealer. Three of the scrolls were bought by an archaeologist; the other four made their way to the USA. They returned to Israel eight years later. Meanwhile, scholars around the world heard about the scrolls and flocked to Jerusalem to study them.

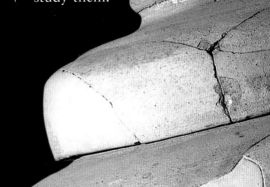

The Dead Sea Scrolls are displayed in a specially built museum called the **Shrine of the Book.** *The dome-shaped building is partly underground to represent the cave where the scrolls were found. The scrolls are on show for only six months at a time. Experts are trying to protect them from humidity, temperature changes and pollution.*

INSIGHT INTO JEWISH LIFE

The Dead Sea Scrolls are a collection of Jewish documents written in Hebrew and Aramaic, the everyday language in the region 2,000 years ago. Some are copies of books in the Bible; some are commentaries on the Bible texts; others describe the beliefs, rituals and political life of Jews at that time.

ANCIENT BIBLE TEXTS

The scrolls were extremely fragile, and no wonder: they were 2,000 years old. Scholars studied them carefully. *Eureka!* They found that they were sections of an ancient copy of the Old Testament, 1,000 years older than any known Hebrew Bible. There was huge excitement. Further searches were carried out in the caves around Qumran, and thousands more pieces of parchment were found. Scholars have spent years piecing them together and interpreting the ancient texts.

HIDDEN FROM THE ROMANS

No one knows the exact truth behind the Dead Sea Scrolls, but most scholars believe that they were written by a Jewish group called the Essenes, who lived at Qumran about 2,000 years ago. Expecting an attack by their Roman rulers, they may have stowed their library in pottery jars and hidden these inside the caves. Twenty centuries later, the texts are on display in Jerusalem, in a museum known as the Shrine of the Book. Perhaps, as scholars continue to study them, we will learn more about the Essenes and their ancient texts.

DEAD SEA SCROLLS

The story of the discovery of the scrolls captured the world's imagination. The texts themselves provide an insight into Jewish life and culture from about 200BCE to CE70. They offer glimpses of the turbulent times leading up to and during the life of Jesus. As a result, they are of great interest to Jewish and Christian scholars.

These pottery jars are similar to those that held the Dead Sea Scrolls. The scrolls were found in a cave overlooking the Dead Sea.

An ancient city built in rock

In 1812, a young Swiss traveller called Johann Burckhardt (1784–1817) was travelling in southern Jordan when he heard about a wonderful ruined city hidden in the desert. He believed it was Petra, an ancient Arab trading centre that had long since fallen into ruin. Burckhardt longed to find Petra, but how?

'A rose-red city – half as old as time!'

JOHN WILLIAM BURGON
Biblical scholar (1819–1888)

PETRA
When Burckhardt discovered Petra, he told the world about the city deep inside a desert gorge. Since then, travellers and historians have visited Petra and learned more about the Nabataeans and their world. Today, Petra is a protected site and Jordan's best known tourist attraction.

WHAT WAS PETRA?

About 2,000 years ago, Petra was the capital city of an Arab people known as the Nabataeans. It was a stopping place for the traders who criss-crossed the ancient world. Over the centuries, the trade routes changed and Petra was abandoned.

*The Nabataeans cut hundreds of **tombs** into the hillsides around Petra. The tombs displayed a family's wealth and honoured those who were laid inside.*

The towering facade of El Deir, the Monastery, has been carved out of solid rock

THE RUINS OF PETRA

Petra's ruined buildings are a spectacular sight in the rugged desert setting. Banquet halls, baths, tombs and shrines were chiselled into the cliffs by local craftsmen. Many of the buildings were elaborately carved then plastered and brightly painted. As well as being skilful builders, the Nabataeans were also clever engineers. Using three nearby springs, they designed an ingenious system of pipelines, tanks and reservoirs, which supplied the city's inhabitants with water for crops and livestock, gardens and fountains, and homes and public buildings.

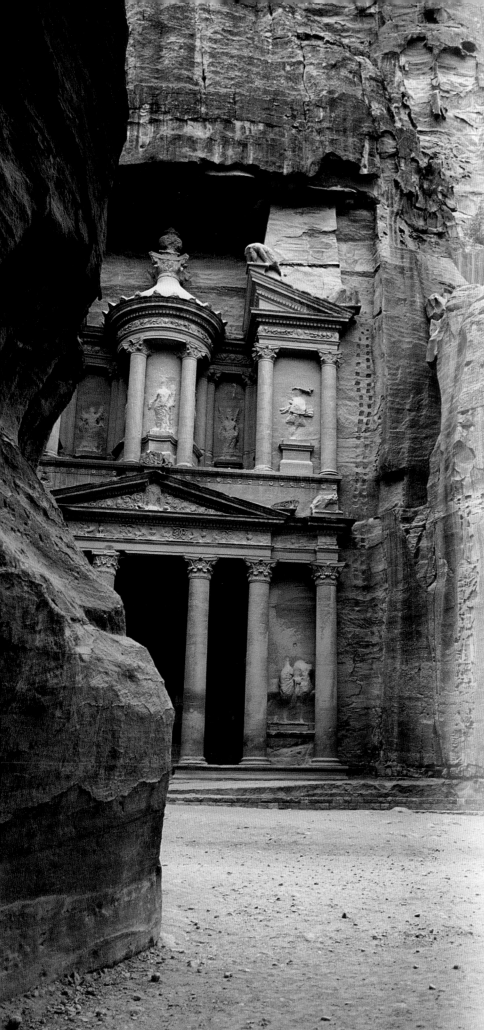

*The first building that Burckhardt would have seen on entering Petra was **El Khazneh, the Treasury**. This ornate, pillared building, is more than 45m tall. It was carved by men who were clearly as skilled at climbing as they were at carving! The building is known as the Treasury because of the urn at its top, which is believed to contain great riches.*

BURCKHARDT'S PLAN

By 1812, Petra had not appeared on a map of the region for more than 1,000 years. Burckhardt knew that if he was going to find the city, he would need a local guide. But the region was dangerous for visitors and he was afraid of being arrested as a spy. So he came up with an ingenious plan. He disguised himself as a Muslim pilgrim by growing a beard and wearing Arab clothes. He told people that he wanted to make a sacrifice to the prophet Aaron (c.15th–13th century BCE), who was believed to be buried in a tomb near Petra. The plan worked: in a few days Burckhardt had his guide and was on his way.

A DAZZLING SIGHT

After days travelling through the desert, Burckhardt's guide turned from the path and entered a narrow ravine. They walked on between its towering walls until, suddenly, a spectacular building came into view. *Eureka!* They had arrived in Petra. Burckhardt was dazzled by the ancient city, with its elaborate buildings carved into solid sandstone cliffs. He later told the world about his find. But it was two Frenchmen, Linant Bellefonds (1799–1883) and Leon de Laborde (1807–1869), who really put Petra on the map. In 1828, they spent a week sketching the city and then published a volume of drawings. People were amazed, and since then travellers from all over the world have visited the site.

A Hindu temple in the jungle

Between the 9th and 14th centuries CE, a Hindu people called the Khmers ruled over much of southeast Asia. Their capital city, Angkor, contained the greatest Hindu temple ever built. When the Khmer empire collapsed, Angkor and its temple were abandoned in the jungle and forgotten about for hundreds of years – until 1861.

'Grander than anything left to us by Greece or Rome.'

HENRI MAHOUT
Botanist and explorer

Angkor Wat, *the largest religious monument in the world, looms out of the forest. Its five carved towers represent the peaks of Mount Meru, the mythological home of the gods, and centre of the Hindu universe.*

! ANGKOR WAT
Mahout's discovery of Angkor Wat brought an architectural masterpiece to the world's attention. The ruined city is a rich resource for historians, providing a unique insight into the Khmer empire and the everyday life of the Khmers.

THE BOTANIST
French botanist Henri Mahout was exploring a remote area of northern Cambodia when he heard tales of a lost city in the jungle. Intrigued, he persuaded a local missionary to guide him to the place. Travelling first by canoe and then on foot, they finally reached some ancient ruins. Great gateways, carved walls and ornate terraces were overgrown by trees and vines. *Eureka!* Mahout had discovered Angkor and its long-lost temple.

WHAT WAS ANGKOR?
Mahout did not realize the full size and magnificence of what he had found. At its peak, Angkor, which means 'the city', covered a huge area with an intricate network of roads, causeways and irrigation canals. Great stairways led up to a series of terraces, where vast temples and palaces rose up towards the sky. The greatest of the temples was Angkor Wat.

The face of Avalokiteshvara, a Buddhist deity, carved in the wall

For 600 years, the vast temple of **Angkor Wat** lay hidden in the jungle of northern Cambodia. When it was discovered, archaeologists stripped the forest from the temple ruins, uncovering porches and walkways with carved balustrades. Paths were cleared around the ancient complex and a road was built from the nearby town of Siem Reap. Years of restoration work still lie ahead.

FINE STONE CARVINGS

The temple of Angkor Wat was built in the 12th century in honour of the Hindu god Vishnu. But it was ransacked in 1177 and part of it had to be rebuilt. This time it was dedicated to the Buddha. It is surrounded by 4km of walls, which are covered in carvings from Hindu and Buddhist mythology. Other wall carvings depict the Khmers working, hunting, tending their animals or riding elephants into battle.

ANGKOR WAT RESTORED

On his return to France, Mahout told the authorities about his discovery. At the time, Cambodia was a French colony, and the government sent teams of archaeologists and scholars to begin restoration work at the site. Cambodians and visitors from around the world began to visit Angkor and marvel at the ruins. Sadly, Angkor Wat was 'lost' again in the early 1970s during a bitter civil war. But today, the site has reopened and the visitors have returned.

Precious cargo under the sea

In the mid 1980s, a Vietnamese fisherman was at work in the South China Sea. He was amazed when, instead of the usual red snappers, he caught something else on his line. It was a concreted lump of iron containing several pieces of blue and white porcelain. The china looked old, and the fisherman thought it might be valuable. He had no idea what it was doing in the sea.

A GOOD CATCH

The man was fishing 160km off the coast of south Vietnam, near the province of Vung Tau. He had always had good catches here, but his latest catch was even better than those. The fisherman went back several times to the area. He hooked more and more pieces of porcelain and sold them to antique dealers for high prices. But eventually the Vietnamese authorities heard about the porcelain and decided to investigate. A salvage company began work in 1990. *Eureka!* Divers found an old Chinese trading ship, known as a lorcha, lying on the seabed. Thousands of pieces of porcelain lay in and around the remains of the hull.

The Vietnamese fisherman hooked up only a small part of the ancient cargo. Divers from the salvage team found thousands of pieces of porcelain covered by sand and shells. The wreck was an old Chinese trading ship about 34m long and 10m wide. It lay in 35m of water.

FAMOUS PORCELAIN

The porcelain found on the Vung Tau wreck was made around the time of the Chinese emperor Kan Xi (1662–1722), the third emperor of the Ching dynasty. It was made from the finest clay, and the elegant pieces, with their blue and white designs, were very popular in the great houses of 17th-century Europe. The craze for Chinese goods at that time, known as 'China mania', led to a highly profitable trade. Teapots, goblets and other pieces were specially designed by Chinese craftsmen for the European market.

Some of the porcelain from the Vung Tau wreck

THE WRECK

Coins found at the site helped the divers to date the ship to about CE1690. Its timbers were burnt, suggesting it sank as the result of a fire – perhaps started by pirates, lightning or accident. The lorcha, like many other ships at the time, was probably sailing along the coast on its way from China to the island of Java. Here, its cargo, bound for Holland, would have been transferred to another ship. Instead, it sank with the lorcha to the ocean floor.

THE CARGO

The divers came across all sorts of goods that had been part of the lorcha's cargo, including kitchenware, bamboo combs, inkstands, tweezers and dice. But the most precious pieces of cargo were the porcelain items, many of them miraculously found intact. In total, about 48,000 pieces were recovered. Of these, thousands went to museums in Vietnam, and 28,000 pieces were taken to Amsterdam, Netherlands, where they were auctioned in 1992. They sold for nearly £4 million!

VUNG TAU WRECK

The discovery of the wreck and its precious cargo was an exciting find for historians. It provided information not only about a 300-year-old cargo ship, but also about Chinese porcelain and the trading links that existed at that time between China and Europe. Visitors to museums in Vietnam are able to see the beautiful porcelain and learn about its fascinating story.

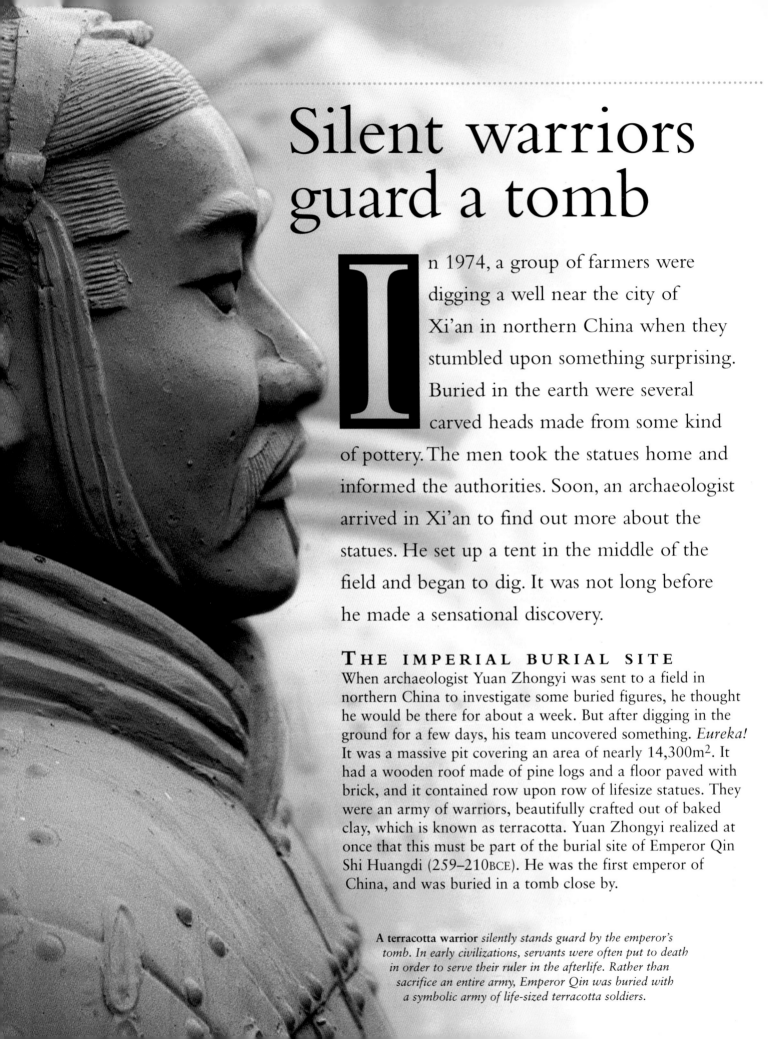

Silent warriors guard a tomb

In 1974, a group of farmers were digging a well near the city of Xi'an in northern China when they stumbled upon something surprising. Buried in the earth were several carved heads made from some kind of pottery. The men took the statues home and informed the authorities. Soon, an archaeologist arrived in Xi'an to find out more about the statues. He set up a tent in the middle of the field and began to dig. It was not long before he made a sensational discovery.

THE IMPERIAL BURIAL SITE

When archaeologist Yuan Zhongyi was sent to a field in northern China to investigate some buried figures, he thought he would be there for about a week. But after digging in the ground for a few days, his team uncovered something. *Eureka!* It was a massive pit covering an area of nearly 14,300m^2. It had a wooden roof made of pine logs and a floor paved with brick, and it contained row upon row of lifesize statues. They were an army of warriors, beautifully crafted out of baked clay, which is known as terracotta. Yuan Zhongyi realized at once that this must be part of the burial site of Emperor Qin Shi Huangdi (259–210BCE). He was the first emperor of China, and was buried in a tomb close by.

A terracotta warrior silently stands guard by the emperor's tomb. In early civilizations, servants were often put to death in order to serve their ruler in the afterlife. Rather than sacrifice an entire army, Emperor Qin was buried with a symbolic army of life-sized terracotta soldiers.

Qin Shi Huangdi, first emperor of China and founder of the Qin Dynasty

THE EMPEROR

Emperor Qin Shi Huangdi was a major figure in Chinese history – a leader, conqueror and ruthless tyrant. He successfully united six warring states into the land we know today as China. As soon as he became emperor, Qin ordered 700,000 slave-labourers to begin working on the tomb in which he would one day be buried, and he commanded craftsmen to make a terracotta army to protect him in the afterlife.

THE EXCAVATION

Archaeologists continued digging at the site. In 1976, they found a second pit, and then two further pits. One of the pits was empty, but the three others contained, in total, nearly 8,000 statues. The archaeologists faced a huge task, and in order to protect the fragile figures, they refilled the new pits temporarily. Since then, two of the pits have been excavated. The figures have been displayed at Qin Shi Huangdi's Museum, which was built near the site. It is now one of the greatest tourist attractions in the world.

TERRACOTTA ARMY

The discovery of the terracotta warriors has brought a unique work of art to the world's attention. The fine detail of the figures provides historians with a rich library of information about the early years of the Chinese empire, and the discovery of his army has provided Emperor Qin Shi Huangdi with the glory and immortality he desired.

Originally painted in bright colours, this **terracotta archer** has faded and lost his wooden crossbow. Other members of the army include officers, cavalrymen and charioteers with chariots and fine horses. Tall, well-proportioned and physically alert, the warriors look as if they are about to go into battle. Their faces are intelligent, resourceful and sincere. This is an emperor's ideal army – one that will defend him to the death!

MAKING THE WARRIORS

Each warrior in the terracotta army is a unique individual and can be distinguished from all the others. Their heads were made from one of about 12 different moulds, and then the eyes and noses were sculpted by hand. Beards, moustaches, hairstyles and headgear helped to create an individual appearance, while arms, legs and armour added further variety. After firing, the figures were painted and given bronze swords and wooden scabbards, crossbows and spears.

Part of the terracotta army

Hoaxes and frauds

The world of discoveries is always open to
question because some finds are not what they
seem. How do you distinguish the genuine from
the fake and the insignificant from an authentic
gem? After proudly announcing a major new
discovery, some experts have faced embarrassment
when the discovery that so excited them was
exposed as a fake. Other experts have missed valuable
genuine artefacts right under their noses. The
identity of a new discovery is easy to mistake, and
even some of the world's most respected scientists
and institutions have been taken in by the sheer
ingenuity and daring of these impressive fakes.

Famous portrait of a president

From time to time, the art world makes interesting and profitable discoveries. Long-lost pictures by famous artists suddenly turn up in dusty attics and forgotten cupboards, or are found hanging unrecognized in antique shops or salerooms. In 1989, a British art dealer was in New York, looking for some interesting paintings. Suddenly, across a saleroom, a familiar portrait caught his eye.

THE SALEROOM

Gavin Graham was visiting the USA, hunting for new pictures for his London gallery. There was an auction of American art coming up at a New York dealer's, and Graham went along to see what was for sale. He was not expecting to find a bargain. He assumed American dealers would bid for work by good American artists, which would push up the price.

This portrait of George Washington is known as the **Gibbs-Channing-Avery portrait.** *It is one of 18 similar works by Gilbert Stuart known as the Vaughan group. It is a copy of an original portrait by Stuart, painted in 1795.*

A portrait of George Washington is reproduced on the USA's 1-dollar bill. It is based on one of Gilbert Stuart's portraits, painted in about 1796.

PAINTING WASHINGTON'S PORTRAIT

The rediscovered portrait of George Washington was one of Stuart's copies of a portrait he painted during a live sitting. This took place at the end of Washington's second term as president, when his political career was ending, and just three years before his death. Stuart asked Washington to sit for him so that he could paint his face more accurately. He used a model when he painted the body. Washington disliked sitting for portraits but he did it out of a sense of duty. He looks like a typical 18th-century gentleman in a black velvet suit. His white hair is powdered and tied back, in the fashion of the day.

THE PORTRAIT

About 200 pictures were to be auctioned, but only one caught Graham's eye. It was a painting of George Washington (1732–1799), the first president of the USA. Art experts know that the official portraits of Washington were painted by Gilbert Stuart (1755–1828). Stuart copied most of these from his original portraits. Lesser known, less talented artists had also painted thousands of copies of the portraits, and the painting that Graham saw for sale was described as one of these. But Graham was not so sure. Looking at it carefully, he judged it had real quality, and, at the auction the following day, he bought it for about £2,000.

THE DISCOVERY

Back in London, Graham sent his picture to an art expert for a thorough investigation. *Eureka!* The painting was one of Gilbert Stuart's portraits of Washington, painted in 1796. It had been commissioned by James Madison (1751–1836), the fourth president of the USA, and later given to his private secretary. The painting had been passed down through the family, but in recent years had been 'lost'. Graham, of course, was delighted with the news. Now that its true identity was revealed, the painting was worth more. It was sold to an American gallery for £250,000.

! PORTRAIT OF GEORGE WASHINGTON

The discovery of one of Gilbert Stuart's portraits was a success story for Graham. Described in a saleroom catalogue as an unremarkable copy, the portrait made Graham a handsome profit. One of the USA's most famous paintings is now correctly identified, properly cared for and returned to its country of origin.

Discovery of an ancient skull

Charles Dawson (1864–1916) was a solicitor and amateur archaeologist. In 1912, he found some fossilized human remains in a gravel pit in Piltdown, Sussex, England. The discovery was greeted with great excitement. Some experts believed the fossils belonged to a new species – a 'missing link' between apes and humans.

WHAT DID IT MEAN?

Eureka! Woodward believed that the human skull bones and the ape-like jaw belonged to a prehistoric human being, which he called *Eoanthropus dawsoni*. Some scientists thought the bones belonged to different species of animals. But Woodward argued that they must belong to one species because they looked so similar in colour and age, and were found so close together. Also, the flat teeth were typical of humans, not apes, which suggested they belonged with the human skull bone. This was undeniably true, and Woodward's views held the day.

THE 'DISCOVERY'

The fragments that Dawson found in the pit at Piltdown included skull bones, teeth and flint tools. He took them to Arthur Smith Woodward (1864–1944) at London's Natural History Museum. Woodward was so interested in them that he joined the excavation at Piltdown. Soon, more ancient animal remains were found. The most significant of these was a fragment of an ape-like jawbone with two flat, molar teeth.

PILTDOWN MAN
Piltdown Man was one of the longest-running frauds. At the time, the ancient skull bones and jawbone were believed to be the oldest human remains ever found anywhere in the world. The case wasted years of scientists' time. However, it taught them to be sceptical and to investigate data carefully.

Dawson *(left)* and Woodward *(right) sieve material at the gravel pit, Piltdown.*

The ape-like jawbone of Piltdown Man containing two flat, human-like teeth

*For more than 40 years, **Piltdown Man** was accepted by many British scientists. The prehistoric human being* Eoanthropus dawsoni *appeared in school books and encyclopedias as the missing link between apes and humans.*

DOUBTS ARISE

Years passed, and as more prehistoric human remains were found around the world, so Piltdown Man began to look 'wrong'. While it had a small brain case with an ape-like jaw, the other finds had a larger brain case with a smaller, human-like jaw. In 1953, a South African scientist called Joseph S Weiner (1915–1982) decided Piltdown Man had to be a fraud. Using the latest testing techniques, he and other scientists proved the skull and jaw came from different species and were of different ages. Piltdown Man was a hoax. Who was responsible? Dawson is a prime suspect but no one actually knows.

A 1915 painting showing scientists examining the Piltdown skull

A reconstruction of *Eoanthropus dawsoni*, widely known as Piltdown Man

HOW PILTDOWN WAS EXPOSED

A new test called the fluorine dating method helped to expose the Piltdown hoax. Buried bones absorb fluorine from the soil and the amount increases with time. The fluorine content of the skull fragments revealed that the jawbone and teeth were modern. They had been stained to match the ancient skull. The jaw fragment was later shown to have come from an orang-utan. Microscopic examination of the teeth revealed that they had been filed down to make them look human.

Photographs of a fantasy world

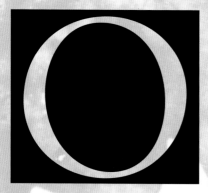

One evening in 1917, in Yorkshire, England, Elsie Wright (1901–1988), aged 16, and her cousin Frances Griffiths (1907–1986), aged nine, came home late for tea. The two girls were scolded, but they had an extraordinary excuse. They told their parents they had been watching fairies. Elsie later produced photographs to support their story, but were they genuine? Were the girls telling the truth?

FAIRY PHOTOS

Elsie Wright and Frances Griffiths spent many hours playing near Cottingley Beck, a stream in the Yorkshire village of Cottingley. This infuriated Frances's mother. When Frances explained that she and Elsie had seen fairies there, her mother became cross. Then Elsie produced photographs. *Eureka!* They showed Frances surrounded by tiny winged people.

THE SENSATION

Elsie's mother was interested in spiritualism (belief in spirits, ghosts and the supernatural). She sent the photos to Edward Gardner (d.1970), a well-known spiritualist, who sent them to a photographic expert. He also contacted fellow spiritualist Arthur Conan Doyle (1859–1930), the author of the Sherlock Holmes stories. They all believed the photos were real, so Conan Doyle published them in a magazine. They caused a sensation!

HOW DID THEY DO IT?

The girls' hoax was inspired by one of Frances's favourite books, called *Princess Mary's Gift Book*. In 1917, when her parents moved from South Africa to Britain, she brought her copy with her. That day in Yorkshire, when Frances was scolded so severely by her mother, Elsie thought her cousin needed cheering up. Being a keen artist, the older girl suggested that they copy fairy drawings out of Frances's book. They copied the figures on to stiff paper and then carefully cut them out. They took the fairies to the stream and arranged them, propped up on hatpins, on the mossy branches of bushes and trees. In some of the photographs the end of the hatpin is clearly visible! Then they took several photographs of themselves with the fairies in different positions and developed them in Elsie's father's darkroom. Little did the two young girls realize that their innocent childhood game would cause such a stir and puzzle the world for 60 years.

Elsie Wright cutting out a paper fairy to demonstrate how she and her cousin faked the photographs of the Cottingley Fairies 60 years earlier

The famous photographs *show Elsie Wright (left) and Frances Griffiths (above) with fairies near Cottingley Beck.*

'I have seen the very interesting photos... they are amazing.'

ARTHUR CONAN DOYLE
Author and spiritualist

THE CONFESSION

Millions of people believed the fairies were real. Many others thought the photos were fake, but whenever the girls were questioned, they always stuck to their story. Years passed and slowly the fuss died down. The girls married and spent many years abroad. It was not until the early 1980s, long after Gardner and Conan Doyle had died, that the truth eventually emerged. Elsie, by then an old lady, confessed that the fairies were fakes. The girls' story had been a silly prank that had snowballed out of control. Fakes or not, the photos never lost their fame. In 1998, after Elsie and Frances had died, they were sold for more than £20,000!

THE COTTINGLEY FAIRIES

The photos of the Cottingley Fairies, said by some at the time to prove the existence of fairies, were some of the most talked-about pictures of the 20th century. It is truly remarkable that, armed with only a camera and a talent for storytelling, two young girls managed to pull off such an extraordinary hoax. Much later, they admitted they had been amazed that people had been taken in by the paper cut-outs.

New painting by a master

In 1937, a Dutch art historian, Abraham Bredius (1855–1946), was asked to examine a recently discovered painting. Bredius was an expert on the Dutch artist Jan Vermeer (1632-1675). When Bredius saw the painting, he was astounded. It was an unknown, genuine Vermeer!

*Genuine paintings by Vermeer, such as **The Lacemaker** (above), were mostly domestic scenes*

Van Meegeren at work on the 'Vermeer' that cleared him at his trial

HOW DID HE DO IT?
Van Meegeren's paintings were technically brilliant. He bought and cleaned 17th-century works of art, leaving a network of cracks in the bottom layer of paint. He used pigments that matched what was available in Vermeer's lifetime and mixed them with synthetic resin instead of oil, so that the paint hardened and appeared very old. He then 'aged' his paintings by baking them.

THE DISCOVERY
As Abraham Bredius studied the newly discovered painting, called *Christ and the Disciples at Emmaus*, he was delighted. He had long believed that, because Vermeer had visited Italy, he must have been influenced by Italian artists and produced paintings on religious themes as well as the domestic scenes for which he was famous. *Eureka!* This new painting, a religious subject in the Italian style, proved that Bredius was right. A Rotterdam museum bought the painting with the help of several huge donations.

A SHOCK ARREST
At this time, many countries in Europe were at war with Germany, and the Netherlands was occupied by the German army. In 1945, as the war was ending, another Vermeer turned up in the collection of a German commander, Hermann Goering (1893–1946). Papers showed that Goering had bought the painting from Dutch artist Hans van Meegeren (1889–1947). Van Meegeren was arrested for collaborating with the enemy – an offence punishable by death.

THE UNKNOWN VERMEER

The van Meegeren case rocked the art world and forced it to change its ways. The intuition of 'experts' was no longer thought a reliable way to evaluate a painting. High-tech tests, such as X-rays and electron microscopy, are now used to identify fakes.

Van Meegeren's painting, entitled **Christ and the Disciples at Emmaus**, *was painted in Vermeer's early style and based on a similar painting, which Vermeer would have seen, by the Italian artist Caravaggio (1573–1610). It fooled art experts until van Meegeren was forced to confess.*

THE COURT CASE

At his trial in 1947, van Meegeren came up with a sensational defence: he had not collaborated with the enemy; he had painted the unknown 'Vermeer' himself! Not only that, but he had also forged the painting of *Christ and the Disciples at Emmaus*. Art historians could not believe their ears. To prove his case, van Meegeren painted another 'Vermeer' while he was in custody. Eventually, he was charged with forgery and sentenced to a year in jail. But one month later, having embarrassed the art world, he suddenly fell ill and died.

'I determined to prove my worth as a painter by making a perfect 17th-century canvas.'

HANS VAN MEEGEREN
Artist

German leader's long-lost diaries

A buzz of excitement swept all around the world when, in April 1983, the German magazine *Stern* made an amazing announcement. Diaries of the German dictator Adolf Hitler (1889–1945) had been discovered and extracts from them would soon be published in the magazine.

THE DISCOVERY

Hitler's newly discovered diaries were made up of 62 handwritten volumes covering the years 1932–1945, before and during the Second World War. Apparently, they had been flown out of Berlin before Hitler's death, but the plane had crashed. The diaries found their way into the hands of *Stern* reporter Gerd Heidemann (b. 1931), who bought the exclusive publishing rights for more than 9 million German marks (about £2.3 million).

Adolf Hitler was an infamous historical figure. Stern hoped that his diaries would reveal his innermost thoughts and feelings.

THE HITLER DIARIES

The Hitler diaries were the most expensive fraud in publishing history. Stern magazine journalists were so desperate to guard the 'scoop', that they failed to do basic checks. They longed too much for the diaries to be real and, along with several eminent historians, they were fooled.

*Controversial historian **David Irving** (b. 1938) declared that the Hitler diaries were fake at a Stern press conference on 25 April 1983. He had originally said they were authentic.*

THE WORLD'S REACTION

Knowing the diaries would attract thousands of readers, many journals rushed to buy the story. The American magazine *Newsweek* and British newspapers *The Times* and *Sunday Times* offered *Stern* a fortune for the right to publish translated extracts. *Eureka!* The diaries were declared authentic, first by leading historian Hugh Trevor-Roper (1914–2003) and then by handwriting experts who compared the script with other Hitler papers. They agreed they were written by the same hand.

THE FORGERY EXPOSED

Suddenly, the story stopped dead in its tracks. Forensic tests proved that the diaries were forgeries after all. The person who had sold them to *Stern* turned out to be Konrad Kujau (1938–2000), a dealer and forger of Nazi memorabilia who had learned to imitate Hitler's handwriting perfectly. Kujau was working in league with Heidemann, who had skimmed off most of *Stern*'s money for himself. The two men were arrested, convicted of fraud and sentenced to four and a half years in prison.

A FORGERY REVEALED

Forensic tests carried out on the diaries proved they were written long after the war. Under ultraviolet light, the paper revealed a whitening agent that came into use only after 1954. Chromatography – a process used to separate dyes – chemically proved that the ink was modern. A further test, which measured the slow evaporation of chloride from the ink, proved that the writing was less than a year old. The diaries even contained historical inaccuracies. They were fakes!

Heidemann (right) faces reporters after the hoax was exposed

Landmark fossil found in China

I n 1999, the owner of a dinosaur museum in the USA saw an interesting specimen at a fossil fair. He thought the fossil was so exciting that he paid nearly £50,000 for it. It was a feathered creature that seemed to be half bird, half dinosaur. Could it be the 'missing link' that proved birds evolved from dinosaurs?

NEW EVIDENCE

The fossil had a head and arms like those of a bird, but the tail, legs and feet of a dinosaur. *Eureka!* It seemed to be the evidence scientists had been hoping to find for 130 years: a species that would prove Huxley's theory that birds evolved from dinosaurs (see page 13). News of the find reached the National Geographic Society. It wanted to be the first to tell the story.

The *Archaeoraptor* fossil, 'found' in a 125-million-year-old slab of rock

FOSSIL FAKES

The Liaoning province of China has produced many exciting fossils, but it also produces fakes. Workers are paid to dig the ground and they earn a bonus if they find a complete fossil. The farmer who found and made the *Archaeoraptor* fossil knew he would get more money if he had a complete specimen. No one knows if he deliberately made a fake, or if he thought he was glueing together pieces of the same creature to make a 'whole'.

'I am 100 percent sure... we have to admit that *Archaeoraptor* is a faked specimen.'

XU XING
Palaeontologist

Scientists began to investigate. They had little information about the fossil because it had been illegally exported from Liaoning in China. With reservations, they confirmed that it was a bird-like creature from the pelvis up and a dinosaur from the pelvis down. They named the new species *Archaeoraptor liaoningensis*. They were still discussing the fossil when *National Geographic* magazine published pictures of the find.

This reconstruction of the 'new species' **Archaeoraptor liaoningensis** *was displayed at National Geographic Society offices in Washington DC. It was viewed by thousands of visitors.*

ARCHAEORAPTOR LIAONINGENSIS
The fossil fake was a humiliation for National Geographic. If it had waited for a full investigation, it would have discovered the truth about the fossil. However, the two parts of the false fossil were both later identified as important new species in their own right.

EXPOSED
Then, in Liaoning province, a Chinese palaeontologist, Xu Xing, discovered the counterslab of the fossil – the other half of the rock in which the fossil was found, which showed its mirror image. The tail in the counterslab was the same, but the rest of the body was different. The fossil in the USA was a fake – the tail had been glued to another fossil. Xu Xing telegrammed *National Geographic* to tell them the bad news.

Index

Acknowledgements

The publisher would like to thank the following for permission to reproduce their material. Every care has been taken to trace copyright holders. However, if there have been unintentional omissions or failure to trace copyright holders, we apologize and will, if informed, endeavour to make corrections in any future edition.

Key: *b* = bottom, *c* = centre, *l* = left, *r* = right, *t* = top

1 Mary Evans Picture Library; 2–3 National Geographic Image Collection/Kenneth Garrett; 4–5 Bettman/Corbis; 6 Dr Robert Ballard; 8–9 Natural History Museum, London; 10*tr* Natural History Museum, London; 10–11 Warren Photographic; 11*cr* Natural History Museum, London; 12*bl* Natural History Museum, London; 13 Warren Photographic; 14 Chris Lisle/Corbis; 15*tr* & 15*c* SPL/Silkeborg Museum, Denmark, Munoz-Yague; 16 Corbis; 18*l* SPL/Sinclair Stammers; 19*tl* & 19*tr* South African Institute for Aquatic Biodiversity courtesy of SAIAB; 19*b* SPL/Peter Scoones; 20*bl* Francis G. Mayer/Corbis; 20*c* Bettman/Corbis; 21*bl* The Image Bank © Getty Images; 21*r* Terry Whittaker, Frank Lane Picture Agency/Corbis; 22 Bool Dan/Corbis Sygma; 23*tl* Advertising Archive/RKO; 23*r* Gavriel/Corbis; 24–25 Christie's Images/Corbis; 26 Bettman/Corbis; 27*tr* HIP/The British Museum; 27*cr* Polak Matthew/Corbis Sygma; 27 *bc* Lowell Georgia/Corbis; 28*c* Bat Conservation International courtesy of © Merlin D. Tuttle; 28*bl* Lowell Georgia/Corbis; 30*bl* & 30*tr* Galaxy Pictures/NOAA; 31*b* Galaxy Pictures/NOAA; 31*cr* Ralph White/Corbis; 32*l* Bettman/Corbis; 33*tl* Bettman/Corbis; 33*b* David Batterbury, Eye Ubiquitous/Corbis; 34*bl* Hulton Getty; 35*t* Bettman/Corbis; 35*cr* Getty Images/Taxi; 36*b* Nik Wheeler/Corbis; 37*tc* Art Archive/Orleans House Gallery; 37*cl* Bettman/Corbis; 37*bl* Corbis; 38*tl* Natural History Museum, London; 38*b* Dave G. Houser/Corbis; 39 Art Archive/Bibliothéque des Arts Décoratifs Paris/Dagli Orti; 40*bl* Getty Images/Stone; 41*c* Christie's Images/Corbis; 41*tr* Art Archive/Muse Cernuschi Paris/Dagli Orti; 42–43 Historical Picture Archive/Corbis; 44*cl* National Geographic Image Collection/Hiram Bingham; 45*cl* Wolfgang Kaehler/Corbis; 45*r* Craig Lovell/Corbis; 46*bl* Leonard de Selva/Corbis; 46*tr* Ralph White/Corbis; 48*bl* Archivo Iconografico, S.A./Corbis; 49*t* & 49*br* Pierre Vauthey/Corbis Sygma; 50*b* HIP/The British Museum; 51*tr* Mary Evans Picture Library; 51*c* Gianni Dagli Orti/Corbis; 52*bl* Art Archive/Pharaonic Village, Cairo/Dagli Orti; 53*cl* Sandro Vannini/Corbis and Vanni Archive/Corbis; 53*r* National Geographic Image Collection/Kenneth Garrett; 54*bl* David Rubinger/Corbis; 54*tr* West Semitic Research/Dead Sea Scrolls Foundation/Corbis; 55*b* HIP/The British Museum; 55*r* Richard T. Nowitz/Corbis; 56*bl* Alison Wright/Corbis; 56*cr* Alan Towse, Ecoscene/Corbis; 57*c* Alison Wright/Corbis; 58*b* Kevin R. Morris/Corbis; 59*tl* Paul A. Souders/Corbis; 59*cr* Luca I. Tettoni/Corbis; 61*tc* Hallstrom Holdings courtesy of Michael Flecker; 62*l* Keren Su/Corbis; 63*tl* HIP/The British Museum; 63*cr* Asian Art and Archaeology, Inc./Corbis; 63*bc* Bridgeman Art Library; 64–65 Bettman/Corbis; 66*bl* Joseph Sohm, Visions of America/Corbis; 67*l* Francis G. Mayer/Corbis; 68*cr* & 68*br* Natural History Museum, London; 69*cr* Natural History Museum, London/The Geological Society; 70 Bettman/Corbis; 71 HIP/NMPFT; 72*bl* Bettman/Corbis; 72*tr* Francis G. Mayer/Corbis; 73 Museum Boijmans van Beuningen, Rotterdam; 74*c* Bettman/Corbis; 75*tl* Focal Point Publications courtesey of © David Irving; 75*br* Bettman/Corbis; 76*bl* & 77 National Geographic Image Collection/O. Louis Mazzatenta; 78–79 Natural History Museum, London; 80 Chris Lisle/Corbis.

The publisher would like to thank the following illustrators: Gino d'Achille 6; Jurgen Ziewe 16–17, 28–29, 46–47, 60–61, 68–69.